The Girls' Schools

by the same author

★

EDUCATION FOR GIRLS

THE
GIRLS' SCHOOLS

The Future of the Public
and Other Independent Schools for Girls
in the Context of State Education

by
KATHLEEN
OLLERENSHAW

FABER AND FABER
24 Russell Square
London

*First published in mcmlxvii
by Faber and Faber Limited
24 Russell Square London WC1
Printed in Great Britain by
Billing and Sons Limited
Guildford, Surrey
All rights reserved*

Contents

Contents

Tables

Tables

Preface

Forty-one years ago, on a Wednesday morning, 5th May, 1926, in the first week of the General Strike, a new girl filling a casual midyear vacancy stood at the end of the row of the lowest form of a great girls' public boarding school, St Leonards School, St Andrews, Fife. I had been driven to Scotland from Manchester the previous day in our first family car—a considerable venture we thought—my parents and I of one mind that to be present on the first day of term was all-important. Four out of five of the girls at that time came from south of the border, and because of the strike not more than half had arrived. I therefore had an exceptionally easy and relaxed introduction to boarding-school life.

I was happy at school; the successes that I had came only gradually and were through trying very hard rather than through flair, except perhaps in my own subject, mathematics, which I loved and in which I had had an excellent grounding in a famous day preparatory school in Manchester, Lady Barn House. This book is my tribute to my two schools and to all who taught me.

KATHLEEN OLLERENSHAW

June, 1967

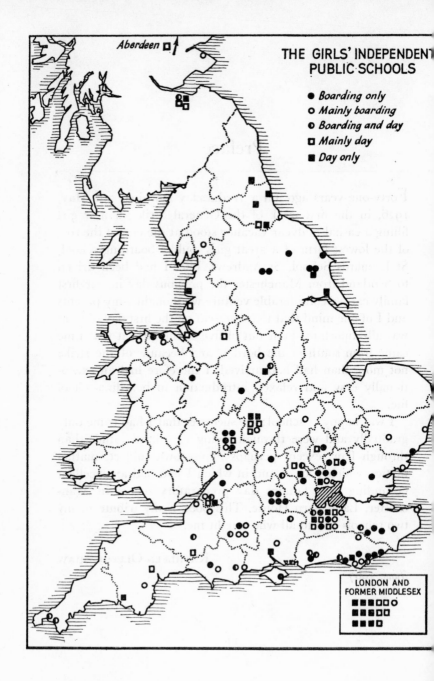

THE GIRLS' INDEPENDENT
PUBLIC SCHOOLS

● Boarding only
○ Mainly boarding
◐ Boarding and day
□ Mainly day
■ Day only

Aberdeen

LONDON AND
FORMER MIDDLESEX

Introduction

In December, 1965, the Government set up a Public Schools Commission under the chairmanship of Sir John Newsom 'to advise on the best way to integrate the public schools into the State system of education'. For the purpose of the Commission, public schools are defined as those independent schools now in membership of the Headmasters' Conference, the Governing Bodies' Association or the Governing Bodies' of Girls' Schools Association. There are about 51,000 boys* and about 38,500 girls of secondary school age in these schools. They have relatively large sixth forms, but only 2·5 per cent of boys and 2 per cent of girls in the 13-year-old age group in the United Kingdom are in the schools which come within the terms of reference of the Commission.

The boys' public schools, commonly thought of as 'The Public Schools', have had their case stated many times. Less is known about the girls' public schools as a whole, largely because they are not at the centre of controversy and do not excite the same envy as do the more famous of the boys' schools. The girls' schools have a different historical background. For this and other important reasons fundamentally different arguments apply about public schools and boarding schools for boys and for girls.

In this book I shall deal with the present and what can be foreseen of the future rather than with the past. My statistics come from the files of the Governing Bodies of Girls' Schools Association and from the Reports of the

* Kalton, G. *The Public Schools: A Factual Survey*, London: Longmans Green, 1966.

13

Introduction

Department of Education and Science, the Girls' School Year Book and the Education Committees Year Book. More particularly, copies of the completed general questionnaire sent to the girls' schools by the Public Schools Commission have been made available to me, and I am most grateful to the headmistresses who have written giving me permission to use the wealth of information contained in them. I am grateful, too, to friends who have criticized my manuscript and given me invaluable help and advice.

I am chairman of the Governing Bodies of Girls' Schools Association but I write here entirely in my private capacity. My views in no way purport to be those of the Association, and even less to be those of governors, headmistresses, past or present pupils or friends of any member school.

Much of what I describe is drawn from personal experience, from conversations with young people and from close knowledge of many schools—as a pupil myself, as a parent whose son and daughter have both attended public boarding schools and as a visitor to many others. I have not hesitated to venture opinions, fears and hopes about the future of the public schools in the light of my day-by-day work as an elected member of a local education authority and my total commitment to the cause of improving state education at all levels.

CHAPTER ONE

Girls' Education
and the Public Schools Commission

EARLY MOTIVATION

A man's greatness, it has been said, may be measured by the length of time after his death during which his work and thought prevail unchallenged. Euclid should perhaps receive the accolade, for over two thousand years elapsed before new geometries were developed: Isaac Newton in the physical sciences would be a runner-up. Among women, Florence Nightingale leaps to mind with her posthumous dominance until very recent years over ideas on nursing and nurses. In girls' education, especially in relation to the girls' public schools, Frances Buss who founded the North London Collegiate in 1850 and Dorothea Beale who became head-mistress of the Ladies' College at Cheltenham in 1857 share, on this criterion, unmatched fame.

This book may now be fairly said to have begun: for according to Sir John Newsom, the chairman of the Public Schools Commission and himself an authority on the history of girls' education, no one can write a serious work on this subject without bringing in the two 'Miss B's'. Their ideas set the pattern of girls' secondary education for the second half of the last century. They had both been among the first students at Queen's College for Women which had opened in Harley Street in 1848 in a house next door to the Governors' Benevolent Institution, itself founded in 1841 to assist 'ladies in temporary distress'.*

The great movement to provide boarding schools for girls from middle-class homes began only a hundred years ago, but some of the girls' public schools are very old foundations —Christ's Hospital Girls' School, Hertford, has a history going back to 1552—and the girls' schools founded before 1902 are among the leading girls' direct grant† and public schools of today. These schools are now facing a serious crisis. The growth of the provision of secondary education for all, in which the public schools led the way, and the shape which secondary education is developing threatens to engulf them; they will have to adapt to survive.

In *The Education of Girls* Sir John Newsom wrote, 'In the final victory of the egalitarians, the names of Frances Buss, Emily Davies and Dorothea Beale will forever be commemorated. For they created the first, or almost the first, educational institutions since the Middle Ages in which girls were able to enjoy a curriculum which was practically identical with their brothers'.' He went on to say, 'As far as I can gather from their own evidence and that of their biographers, the learned ladies . . . never stopped to think whether the educational opportunity for which they appealed had been designed to meet the needs of women'.

The argument about what is the best or right education for girls and whether it should be different in essentials from that of boys has raged for several centuries and still rages. The pendulum swung from the one extreme of total differen-

---

* Kamm. Josephine *How Different from Us.* London: Bodley Head, 1958; *Hope Deferred*, London: Methuen, 1965.
† See Glossary and Chapter Four.

tiation to the other of as great similarity as possible for girls—at least for the ablest—as for boys. Just where the balance should lie is still not clear, but surely this must be judged afresh by each generation in turn and as ideas alter about the role of women in adult society, at work and in the home. Now that the battle for equality of educational opportunity for girls is largely though not wholly won, we are more prepared to concentrate on the individual and varying needs of all pupils, boys and girls; we have switched to a new battle ground.

Before the new public schools for girls were established in the second half of the nineteenth century, almost the only formal education available to them except in a few ancient endowed schools was given in the home or in finishing schools of which it was said in 1868 that 'the education given at girls' schools is partly answerable for the vapid characters and frivolous pursuits of idle women'. The pioneers of girls' secondary education were well ahead of the state, so that traditions which have since permeated the girls' grammar schools and other selective schools in the state system were taken over from the early public schools. The pioneers were not particularly concerned with girls' potential earning power or with a girl's chances in the marriage market, although these were incidental benefits of better education, but with equal opportunity with boys for intellectual development hitherto denied to all but the most fortunately placed or the really exceptional girls. To quote from *The Year Book of Education*, 1932, 'They were concerned with one thing and one thing only—to make available for girls the best education then known. They wanted to learn, and to enable other girls and women to learn, Latin and Greek and mathematics, not because boys learnt them, but because they were in themselves good things to learn.' In 1864, Emily

Davies, who was the founder of Girton College, Cambridge, claimed, 'We are not encumbered by theories about equality and inequality of mental power in the sexes. All we claim is that the intelligence of women, be it great or small, shall have full and free development. And we claim it not specifically in the interest of women, but as essential to the growth of the human race.'

These high sentiments were somewhat obscured in the struggles which followed. To obtain the educational opportunity they sought—in particular, to gain entry to the universities and the professions—women had to demonstrate to the men in authority that they were capable of equal academic achievement. The abler girls in a public school were expected almost as a moral obligation to train for teaching or, if they did not want to teach, to try to break into other professions. The great fight of Elizabeth Garrett Anderson (1836–1917), who became the first woman doctor to have her name entered on the Medical Register, although it was not successful, paved the way for other women who followed her. If these girls chose to marry, as most did, then they were encouraged to give themselves unstintedly to social work and good causes. But if those who succeeded in blazing the trail to the universities accepted offers of marriage this was regarded as letting down the side. There was a marriage bar in teaching (which, incredibly, was still in force in some parts of the country until the second world war) and in most of the other professional and semi-professional occupations which were gradually being prised open by qualified women. Educated women had to make the harsh choice between marriage and a career—one or other, but not both. The demographic balance between the sexes accentuated this. Whereas now there are rather more than 106 unmarried men to every 100 unmarried women in the main marrying age groups (taken as $17\frac{1}{2}$ to 45 for men and 15 to $42\frac{1}{2}$ for women), before the war there were about 80 unmarried men to every 100 unmarried women in these age groups. Many women who would today most certainly be married in their twenties or earlier chose a career. Their sacrifice was great and rarely given full credit by most of the women who married; mutual envy and sometimes lack of true respect between the two groups was common. The idea grew that intellectually able women were necessarily unmarriageable blue-stockings, and this created in the minds of many career women themselves a defensive and compensatory sense of superiority, which remained characteristic until the rise of the post-war generation of girls who regard marriage as certain and who confidently expect to be able to combine work and marriage if they so wish.

The motives which influenced the development of the girls' public schools were fundamentally different from those affecting the boys' schools. The new boys' public schools of the late nineteenth century were founded to extend the opportunity of existing public school education to a larger number of boys, the sons of the rising middle class professional and merchant families. Headmasters of some of the boys' schools, notably Thring of Uppingham and Sanderson of Oundle, introduced ideas which were considered very advanced at the time—more science, less insistence on the classics, more practical work for the academically less able boys (and, indeed, at Oundle for every boy—even the classical sixth), drama and music as vehicles of education, and other innovations.

These ideas fitted well with the enlightened thinking of the day among the leaders in the promotion of secondary education for girls. But the girls' schools had an additional mission. They had to establish the academic capabilities of women in

19

competition with men and they had to do this with the approval and support of Victorian parents—in particular of Victorian fathers. Rules of behaviour and deportment were therefore strict, but they were not especially rigorous judged by the standards of the day, and headmistresses and staff, being educated women of impeccable upbringing and background themselves, were usually humanitarian. For many girls at the public boarding schools conditions were less hard, and individual girls' needs often far better understood and catered for at school than at home. Teasing and ragging of new girls was not acceptable in the school which I attended. Prefects were expected to help and to look after newcomers even if they did insist on rules being learnt and kept. Bosom friendships and cliques were actively discouraged; so were grand passions. Corporal punishment in the girls' public schools was almost unknown, although caning the hand was common in the maintained* schools (and is still resorted to in some). Organized games were the fashion; they were considered an important way of teaching team spirit and qualities of leadership—and, let it be said, a method unequalled in effectiveness in keeping large numbers of adolescents under the eye of authority, out of mischief, and relatively happily occupied in healthy outdoor exercise.

The public schools as well as the maintained schools are changing. Their original motivation—the need to prove that girls can benefit by an academic secondary education—is now no longer operative. The girls' public schools must stand —or fall—on their merits in a competitive world; a world in which state secondary education, freely available, is itself now setting many of the trends with new courses, new curricula and syllabuses, new methods and techniques of teaching, and, where buildings are new, often with mag-

* See Glossary.

nificent amenities and equipment. We have to judge the situation not by the past, but as it is today and as it is likely to develop in the next ten or twenty years.

THE IMAGE

What then makes parents decide today to send a daughter, usually at considerable expense, to a public school? What are the girls' public schools like today, and what have they to offer which in this swinging, gregarious technological age is still attractive to parents? Boarding education may be sought for its own sake, but not all public schools are boarding schools. Parents may be attracted by the small school when maintained secondary schools tend all to be large or to be becoming large. Classes are usually but not always smaller than in maintained schools, partly because the girls' public schools make great use of part-time staff. Religious education becomes a way of life in some boarding schools which are denominational foundations and is a strong motive for many parents. Quakers and Roman Catholics will make considerable sacrifices to send their children to schools which are of their religious persuasion and this may be a growing incentive when pressures, in this pop era, seem all toward eliminating religious observance of any kind from the maintained schools. Family tradition or some real or supposed social cachet may influence parents' decisions. There will be many reasons and these will differ according to where parents live and according to how the state system itself develops in different parts of the country.

The image of the girls' public boarding schools in TV-soaked eyes can range from that of St Trinians, with its whisky-swigging, hockey-stick-hacking, little horrors, to seminaries for nice girls where daughters can be safely locked up for the greater part of their troublesome teenage years. In fact none of the girls' public schools fit either image. The schools vary widely in size, in character, in the emphasis that they put on this or that aspect of girls' education; but all do the best they can to give a sound academic, practical, physical and spiritual education to the girls in their care, and all of them are subject to modern social and educational pressures and to change.

The mystique attached to the boys' public boarding schools does not apply to the girls' schools. No one really supposes that if the continuance of the girls' public schools only was in question there would now be a Commission to inquire into them. Indeed, the new Commission might be much happier if the issues to be discussed were not blurred by the inclusion of the girls' schools. But inevitably the future of the girls' public schools is firmly linked with that of the boys' schools and what is decided for the boys' schools will directly affect them all.

Although, in their history, the girls' public schools differ in many fundamental ways from the boys' public schools they make a comparable contribution to girls' education as a whole. Their active tradition of preparing girls for higher education and for the professions is of special importance at a time when vacancies for qualified women to serve in posts of high responsibility are increasingly hard to fill. Governors of girls' independent schools and headmistresses are perplexed by present threats of wholesale takeover bids by the state. What are they to say to parents and how are they to plan the development of their schools? What does the future hold for them?

THE COMMISSION

The Public Schools Commission is required to recommend a national plan for integrating the public schools with the maintained sector of education.* No clear definition of what is intended by integration has yet emerged, but close co-operation between the independent and maintained schools to say the least is plainly envisaged. The Commission's task is to suggest *how* close links should be forged. The brief precludes any objective examination of whether or not integration is desired or desirable: this is taken for granted and is part of the present Government's declared education policy. Moreover, the maintained sector into which the Government would like to see the public schools integrated is not the semi-selective arrangement of today with grammar schools, technical schools, modern schools and comprehensive schools all co-existing, but a wholly non-selective 'all-comprehensive' system of secondary education for which plans are now being made. Although some of the girls' public schools take pupils covering a fairly wide spread of academic ability only a few claim or set out to provide a full range of sixth-form courses for really able girls as well as five-year courses for less able girls intending to leave school at 16. Indeed, none of them are large enough to do this economically. A policy decision to eliminate selection based on academic ability, high or low, therefore presents a perhaps crucial difficulty for the public schools, particularly if they are considered in isolation from the rest of the independent schools.

The Newsom Commission is not the first to be set up to report on the public schools. In 1861 a Royal Commission under Lord Clarendon was appointed 'to inquire into the

* The full terms of reference are given in the Appendix.

Revenues and Management of certain Colleges and Schools, and the studies pursued and instruction given therein'. The Clarendon Commission reported in 1864 on the nine leading boys' public schools. The Public Schools Act which followed in 1868 made certain important recommendations about the powers of governing bodies of schools and headmasters, about the curriculum and about methods of selecting pupils. In 1864 another Royal Commission, known as the Schools Inquiry Commission, was appointed to report on those schools which had not come within the scope of the Clarendon Commission. Under the chairmanship of Lord Taunton this Commission's terms of reference included consideration of the secondary education of girls—an important advance for girls.

More recently, in 1942, as a prelude to the Education Act of 1944, the then President of the Board of Education set up a Committee on Public Schools under the chairmanship of Lord Fleming 'to advise him on means whereby the association between the Public Schools and the general educational system of the country could be developed and extended'. Direct grant schools in membership of the Headmasters' Conference or Governing Bodies' Association as well as the equivalent girls' independent and direct grant schools were covered by the terms of reference. The main recommendation of the Fleming Report, published in 1944, fell into two parts, the second of which dealt with the public boarding schools. The suggestion was that the schools should provide up to 25 per cent of their annual admissions to pupils from grant-aided primary schools, the tuition and boarding fees and other expenses to be remitted to parents according to an approved income scale, with total remission where necessary; the scheme was to be sponsored by local education authorities. The schools welcomed these proposals, but the response from local authorities was, and still is, minimal. The difficulties of selecting on educational grounds a very few children from huge primary school populations for special and highly expensive boarding education can seem insuperable even when local authorities have been sympathetic to the idea, which a great many, particularly in the north, are not. Lord Fleming's Committee never faced this problem of how to select the pupils, and in as far as the Report dealt with the public boarding schools it quickly became, and still remains, virtually a dead letter. Meanwhile, the best known public schools continue to flourish despite some grave financial problems and uncertainties, but they are increasingly the subject of strident criticism on the grounds that they are a socially and educationally divisive influence within society.

Only independent schools are included in the remit of the Newsom Commission. Direct grant schools, most of which are members of one or other of these associations, are this time deliberately excluded from the terms of reference, although a few of the leading direct grant schools may in the event be brought in. In general therefore, the Newsom Commission has a narrower field to cover for its principal recommendations than either the Taunton Royal Commission of a hundred years ago or the Fleming Committee of 1942.

The exclusion of the direct grant schools has caused much disappointment, both to these schools themselves and to the independent public schools, with some of which they have much in common. Educationally, the larger independent public day schools are almost indistinguishable from direct grant grammar schools. Moreover, some of the independent public boarding schools have felt that an extension of the direct grant idea might be the best method of bringing them more closely in line with the state system. The Government seem, however, to have prejudged any such proposal by asking local authorities to discuss methods of bringing the direct grant schools in their areas within their own plans for reorganizing secondary education on comprehensive principles.

By the terms of reference of the Newsom Commission, co-educational schools other than the four which are members of the GBA and independent schools concerned largely with pupils of the middle and lower ranges of ability are not a main consideration. The Commission has only 'to recommend whether any action is needed in respect of other independent schools'. The Headmasters' Conference and the Governing Bodies' Association accept in membership only all-boys' schools and a few co-educational schools with strong academic records, all of which must normally prepare boys for universities and other forms of higher education. The Governing Bodies' of Girls' Schools Association similarly accepts only all-girls' schools which have academic sixth forms. A characteristic of the public schools is that all pupils are expected to stay at school until at least 17 years of age.

There are significant differences in the patterns and levels of educational achievement of boys and girls of all abilities after the age of 16. Ideas about careers and training are entirely different. Prospects of marriage, and particularly of early marriage, affect girls' education in a way that has little or no relevance to the education of boys. The new pattern of a short period in employment and then a break of ten or twenty years while raising a family followed by a return to work requires special consideration. Girls develop physically, emotionally and intellectually at a different pace from boys during the critical years of growing up between 12 and 18 as well as while of primary school age.* None the less, the

* Cf. Plowden Report: *Children and Their Primary Schools*. London: H.M. Stationery Office, 1967.

organization of education, at least in the maintained sector, is broadly the same for boys and for girls and requirements for entry for the universities and for the professions are of course the same. Whether or not this is sometimes to the disadvantage of girls is largely irrelevant; it has to be accepted as more or less inevitable.

CO-EDUCATION

Although strong views on the advantages and disadvantages of co-education are held by teachers and parents, particularly by those concerned with boarding education, it has never been a major issue in this country in policy decisions about school provision—actual decisions, whether about building for co-education or single-sex secondary education or about which type of education to choose for a child, are usually taken in the event with other principles uppermost. Grammar schools for boys came first and girls' schools were founded later to give girls an equal opportunity. Most maintained elementary schools were co-educational, and so senior elementary schools which later were translated into secondary modern schools were also usually co-educational. The tendency since 1944 has been to build for co-education, other factors being equal; but when a co-educational grammar school, for example, has become overcrowded and when the site has been too small for expansion of the buildings a second separate school has often been built on a new site and either the boys or the girls have moved over, thus creating two single-sex schools from one that had been co-educational. In 1955, 46 per cent of maintained secondary schools were co-educational; in 1965, this proportion had risen to 56 per cent.

Girls' Education and the Public Schools Commission

There is little or no evidence to show that girls do better or worse in academic work whether in the arts or science subjects when they are in co-educational or single-sex schools, or whether co-education encourages them to stay on longer at school. The published statistics of the Department of Education and Science for staying-on, sixth-form numbers, GCE results and destination of school leavers do not distinguish between those attending co-educational and single-sex schools.

Only four of the schools defined as public schools are co-educational. About 7 per cent of the independent secondary schools recognized as efficient and about 20 per cent of independent 'primary and secondary' recognized as efficient are co-educational, but a majority of these co-educational independent 'primary and secondary' schools are really girls' schools which accept boys in their junior departments only. Arguments about whether co-education or single-sex education is the better are usually based on personal experiences and depend on what educational aim is uppermost in any particular set of circumstances. Most headmasters of unselective schools will say that they prefer co-education on the grounds that this method best educates the 'whole person'— certainly a co-education school makes a better social unit than a single-sex school and the girls may help to 'civilize' the boys. Headmistresses will usually prefer girls' schools for girls. Here is the fundamental dilemma: if social aims predominate, as they must in difficult areas, then probably co-educational schools are 'good for boys and bad for girls'; if academic achievement is the principal aim then it is probably the other way, 'good for girls and bad for boys'.

The main argument for single-sex schools that applies equally for boys and girls is that they develop physically and emotionally at a different pace, particularly at and about the

28

age of puberty, and that their individual needs can best be met by teaching them in segregated groups at least for part of the time during the years of adolescence. Also some parents and headmistresses feel that there is advantage for some girls in their being withdrawn during the school day or at boarding schools for the school term from the emotional turmoil of relationships with boys so that they may develop poise and self-confidence in the somewhat more sheltered atmosphere of a girls' school. Strong advocates of co-education as an educational value in itself will say that this is the 'natural' way of running a school and that problems of adolescence are then met in a normal environment where a real attempt can be made to help boys and girls to resolve them. Co-educational boarding schools, of course, have organizational difficulties, and, in general, they need for success a high degree of maturity of personality in members of staff. There may be many public boarding schools, boys' as well as girls', which would have no objection in principle to widening their recruitment to include pupils of both sexes —but the practical problems would be formidable and a small minority group either of boys or of girls in a school might not achieve desired educational aims. At sixth-form level there may be more gain and fewer problems, and if the sixth-form college idea grows in popularity the assumption is probably that these should normally be co-educational as is most other college education now.

The best solution and that generally adopted is to try to have both co-educational and single-sex schools wherever possible and to allow parents to take their choice. In practice, however much parents may protest that they want, for example, a girls' school for their daughter, if the available girls' school has a poor reputation they quickly change their minds—the criterion of choice first and foremost is for the best school, whatever its designation. New plans for re-organization on comprehensive lines may swing the pendulum further toward more co-educational schools whenever 'twinned' schools for boys and for girls in buildings not too far apart are joined together to form upper and lower departments of one comprehensive school.

Governors and heads of all independent schools are at the present time perplexed by current uncertainties and by the implied threats of possible takeover bids by the state system or by insurmountable taxation. They know that they do a good job, but some re-orientation in the thinking of many 'public schools' people', to invent a new generic term, is clearly necessary.

Informed discussion can take place only where recent developments outside the public schools are properly understood. The next chapters are therefore given to an account of the progress and change since 1944 in the maintained schools and colleges in England and Wales, in the universities and in women's careers and work, with some indication of the trends, conflicts and probable lines of advance in the immediate future.

CHAPTER TWO

The Educational Revolution

GROWTH IN SCHOOL POPULATION

There were 371,000 girls aged 13 attending school in the United Kingdom in 1965 of whom 340,000 were at maintained schools, 11,000 at direct grant schools and 20,000 at independent schools, that is, 91·6 per cent, 3·0 per cent and 5·4 per cent respectively (Table I). The percentages of 13-year-old boys attending maintained, direct grant and independent schools were, rather surprisingly, exactly the same as for the girls. This chapter is largely about this 91·6 per cent of pupils who attend maintained secondary schools.

Until 1902, when secondary education first became a permissible charge on local rates, the only secondary education available for girls was in the independent public boarding and day schools. Two out of three of today's girls' public schools and almost all today's girls' direct grant and voluntary aided schools which provide substantial sixth-form courses were founded before the turn of the century, that is, before local education authorities began to establish secondary schools.

Despite two world wars and the economic depressions of the 1920's and 1930's, steady progress in the state system of education was made. Secondary education in the schools

TABLE I

The number of boys and girls aged 13 and of all ages in January 1965 in all schools in the United Kingdom excluding special schools for the handicapped

	Maintained Schools or Departments		Direct Grant Schools or Departments		Independent Schools or Departments		All Schools or Departments	
		%		%		%		%
Boys aged 13	349,930	91·6	11,354 (5,664*)	3·0	20,790 (10,529*)	5·4	382,074	100
Girls aged 13	335,801	91·6	10,801	3·0	19,948	5·4	366,550	100
Boys and Girls aged 13	685,731		22,155		40,738		748,644	
Boys (all ages)	4,232,026	92·7	86,200	1·9	247,666	5·4	4,565,892	100
Girls (all ages)	4,014,366	92·8	83,694	1·9	229,535	5·3	4,327,595	100
Boys and Girls all ages	8,246,392		169,894		447,201		8,893,487	

Source: *Statistics of Education Part I*, 1965. London: H.M. Stationery Office, 1966.

* The figures in brackets are the number of 'school entrants' to boys' direct grant and independent *public schools* in the school year 1962–63 given in *The Public Schools: A Factual Survey* by Graham Kalton. This indicates that roughly half the boys entering independent secondary schools go to schools defined as public schools. No figures are yet available for girls' public schools separately, but probably about two-fifths of girls entering independent secondary schools go to schools defined as public schools (see Chapter V).

maintained by local authorities was provided for boys and for girls with scrupulous equality. By the end of the second world war, 30 per cent of both boys and girls aged 13 were still attending 'all-age' elementary schools and not receiving any real secondary education, 20 per cent were in grammar schools, and the rest in other forms of secondary schools. The only significant difference in provision for boys and for girls was in secondary technical schools, two out of three of which were boys' schools recruiting at the age of 13 and situated in local technical colleges—an example, not uncommon in the history of British education, of educational theory being made to fit practical expedience. Without the invention of technical schools, these colleges, which catered largely for apprentices and other students following evening courses, would have been standing empty during the daytime.

Progress since 1944 has been remarkable. The first ten years were heavy going; the ravages of war and the unexpectedly large birth-rate immediately afterwards created a situation of almost perpetual crisis. The Education Act of 1944 began a new epoch of educational thought and administration. The President of the Board of Education was restyled Minister of Education in charge of a ministry with considerable powers. Local administration of education was rationalized by abolishing the small local education authorities which provided elementary education only, and by making the county and county borough councils the local education authorities for all forms of public education. The Act laid upon these local authorities the duty of providing secondary education suited to ages, abilities and aptitudes for all children from the age of 11 to 15; the Act also provided for the raising of the school-leaving age to 16 by Order in Council 'as soon as the Minister is satisfied that it has become practicable'. Twenty years passed before Sir Edward Boyle, the then Minister of Education, announced in January, 1964, that the age would be raised to 16 in the academic year 1970–71.

Part III of the 1944 Act required all independent schools to be registered. This section of the Act was not brought into force until 1957 because of pressure of work on Her Majesty's

C

Inspectors. In addition to registration a school may also seek to be 'recognized as efficient'. Recognition requires higher standards than registration only, and consequently leads to higher status, particularly as it entitles a school's teaching staff to belong to the national superannuation scheme. In 1965 there were 551 registered independent girls' schools offering secondary education in England and Wales, of which 410 were recognized as efficient—154 of these are public schools. Recognized schools must be of a standard at least equivalent to that expected of maintained schools and must be large enough to provide a reasonable range of subjects over a three-year course and have adequate teaching staff.*

Regulations made by the Minister under the 1944 Act included a maximum size for ordinary primary school classes of 40 and for any class in a secondary school, 30. These modest aims have still not been complied with, but despite all difficulties achievement has been outstanding; there has been continuous growth—in numbers staying on beyond the school-leaving age; in amenities; in the range of subjects taught and activities undertaken. The number of pupils in maintained primary and secondary schools in England and Wales has risen from just over five million to well over seven million since 1947, but schools have never had to resort to shift working except perhaps temporarily in a few areas. There were 174,000 pupils of 16 in maintained schools in 1965, compared with 64,000 in 1955 and 50,000 in 1950; more than one in every four pupils is now staying on at school until 16 compared with one in six only ten years ago and the number in sixth forms has grown from 60,000 to

* See the Plowden Report, Chapter 27, for a discussion of registered and recognized status in relation to primary schools: *Children and their Primary Schools*. London: H.M. Stationery Office, 1967.

170,000—this with the statutory leaving age still only 15. Although many teachers and administrators have misgivings about the wisdom of undertaking the formidable task of raising the age in 1970–71 while the severe shortage of teachers still persists, the Government is showing a determination to stick to the decision, and active plans are being made to try to ensure success. In the event, whether or not the date is postponed for, say, two years, will probably depend not on educational considerations but on the employment situation. Faced with a choice between 300,000 unemployed young workers or crowded schools, the political answer is obvious.

By 1975 one in six pupils will probably be staying on at school until 17 years of age. Even without any allowances for pupils staying on to 17 as a consequence of raising the school-leaving age, official forecasts show that, with the larger age groups and the trend to stay on, the total number of children in maintained primary and secondary schools in England and Wales is likely to reach over $9\frac{1}{4}$ million in 1975, an increase of nearly $2\frac{1}{4}$ million over the 1965 total compared with an actual increase of 587,000 between 1955 and 1965. This requires a rate of expansion of buildings and in staff in the 1965–75 decade of nearly four times that of the decade just past—a tremendous undertaking which makes present building programmes and plans for increasing the supply of teachers seem alarmingly inadequate.

NURSERY EDUCATION

In two sectors of educational provision the state has made very little progress—nursery education and boarding. Nursery provision for children of 3 to 5 years of age has remained almost unchanged in England since the 1930's* at about 7 per cent of all children under 5. The case for nursery school provision is irrefutable on educational grounds and should be given a high priority in new educational advance. An estimate of the additional expenditure required for England has been given in the Plowden Report as £22 million a year by 1977 and £49 million a year by the time full provision could be achieved after 1980. There is little real hope that the recommendations on this made by Lady Plowden's committee will be implemented unless and until the economic climate changes greatly for the better—meanwhile, the most that local authorities can do is to provide nursery classes wherever there is spare space in primary schools or other buildings suitably adapted, and to give priority to children whose mothers are qualified teachers and who would thereby be enabled to go back to teaching.

LOCAL EDUCATION AUTHORITY BOARDING PROVISION

Local education authorities have for many years provided boarding accommodation in residential special schools for handicapped children, for the physically handicapped, the deaf, blind, partially-sighted, educationally sub-normal and maladjusted, for epileptics and now for psychotic children. Apart from these special schools and short-term residential or holiday camp schools fewer than 150 boarding schools have been established by local authorities in England and Wales and much the greater number of these have been

* See the Plowden Report, Vol. 1. Chapters 9 and 31: *Children and their Primary Schools*. London: H.M. Stationery Office, 1967.

selective schools. Local authority boarding provision for normal children of average and less than average ability is totally inadequate.

The local authorities have, however, also met accepted cases of boarding 'need' in independent boarding schools and in independent and direct grant schools which have boarding houses—and in this way they have been able, at least theoretically, to find suitable courses for children in 'need' of boarding in every category of ability. Criteria for determining the circumstances in which local education authorities might feel under some obligation to provide residential education for children irrespective of levels of ability were formulated in a Ministry of Education report* in 1960.

(i) Cases in which both parents are abroad.
(ii) Cases in which the parents are in England and Wales but are liable to frequent moves from one area to another.
(iii) Cases in which home circumstances are seriously prejudicial to the normal development of the child.
(iv) Cases in which a special aptitude in the child requires special training which can be given to the child only by means of a boarding education.

This report, commonly known as the Martin Report after its chairman Mr L. C. J. Martin, also made recommendations about scales of local authority grants to assist parents according to their income with tuition and boarding fees and other necessary expenses. In 1960 there were 8,499 boarding places (6,378 for boys, 2,121 for girls) available in maintained schools in England and Wales; in addition, local authori-

* Report of the Working Party on *Assistance with the Cost of Boarding Education* (The 'Martin Report'). London: H.M. Stationery Office, 1960.

ties accepted full or part responsibility for the payment of fees for 4,499 boys and 2,426 girls in non-maintained schools.*

In 1965 a working party of the Association of Education Committees prepared a report† on boarding education in which an estimate was made of the number of boys and girls classified in three broad categories of ability for whom local education authorities might require boarding education if it were available, and this notional demand was matched against the willingness of schools to make places available provided that fees were paid. The inquiries of the working party showed a great willingness on the part of all schools of all kinds with boarding accommodation, maintained, direct grant and independent, to co-operate by making places available for children whose parents were assisted with fees by local authorities. The working party concluded that there is enough boarding accommodation available to enable local education authorities to place boys and girls of all categories of ability who are in 'need' of boarding in schools which can cater for them to their education advantage. There was no consideration in this report of the extent of parents' desire for boarding education for their children as distinct from children's 'need'.

The Department of Education and Science is at the present time giving financial support to a full-scale investigation under the direction of Dr Royston Lambert in Cambridge into the value and provision of, and demand for, boarding education in England and Wales. Dr Lambert prepared an interim report‡ for the Public Schools Commission which was published in 1966. He showed that local

* The Martin Report, cit., Appendix II.

† *Boarding Education* (the Alexander Report). London: Association of Education Committees, 1965.

‡ Lambert, R. *The State of Boarding Education*. London: Methuen, 1966.

education authorities took widely and often inexplicably different standpoints in their interpretation of the four criteria of boarding need and that there are extreme diversities and even contradictions of policy about what constitutes 'need' which qualifies for financial assistance. He makes a plea for the recognition by government policy of the state's increasing involvement in secondary boarding education in this country and for more carefully defined and coordinated policies, procedures and provision by local education authorities.

Experience of local education committees indicates that requests for assistance with boarding education are usually laid before members for consideration on merit; the nature of decisions depends very much on the individually held views of committee members or the chairman concerned who will keep within a vaguely defined case-law of precedent. If local education committees suddenly became much more generous in their interpretation of boarding need, if they decided to support parents' requests on the broader grounds of desire for boarding (which a few authorities already do), and if this became widely known, there might well be a new and overwhelming demand which would immediately defeat any hope of meeting it. There is a marked class distinction in the desire for boarding—middle- and upper-class homes have for nearly a hundred years now been attuned to the idea of sending children to boarding schools, whereas parents in lower income groups and in unskilled or semi-skilled occupations have tended to associate boarding schools with either physical or mental handicap or wrong-doing. Any significant extension of local authority boarding provision to meet parental wishes would probably therefore help middle-class parents, at least to begin with, in much larger numbers than parents in lower income groups.

The recent publicity given to boarding school provision is of special significance in the context of the future of the public schools, so many of which are either for boarders only or have some provision for boarders. If government policy in the future is revised to include an acceptance of the desire for boarding education at the secondary stage as a legitimate parental wish which should be met at least in part and as far as is reasonable within the state system of education, then the co-operation of the independent schools which have boarding accommodation would appear to be essential and their continued existence as flourishing and viable institutions in well-kept buildings in the meantime would also appear to be in the best long-term interests of the state system itself, irrespective of other considerations.

SCHOOL BUILDING

Building the schools and training teachers have been the two principal administrative problems of providing for all these extra pupils. Building programmes have been held in check by lack of both money and resources, but when capital funds have been allocated, the construction industry and architects' departments, although sometimes stretched to breaking point, have managed to meet the demands. New school places for nearly four million children, that is for over half of all pupils now in maintained primary and secondary schools in England and Wales, were provided between 1946 and 1965. During the past fourteen years local authorities have built well and they have built economically. In this they have been greatly assisted by the Development Group set up within the Architects and Building Branch of the Department of Education and Science. This Development Group undertakes experiments in new designs and in the use of new building materials and techniques. The Group sometimes builds a complete school or other educational unit in collaboration with a local authority. There are current experiments in 'sixth-form units' and in accommodation for the use of the less able pupils when the school-leaving age is raised. Principles of costing were laid down in 1952 whereby a maximum cost-per-pupil-place and not less than a prescribed minimum amount of teaching area has to be met. This gives some flexibility about cost-per-square-foot and was a useful innovation. The effect of knowing from the beginning the limits of cost within which work must be kept has stimulated ingenuity and inspiration. New thought is all the time given to the fundamental requirements in educational building to match the new approaches to learning and new teaching methods. Revolutionary ideas about the use of space, cutting down on corridors and so on, have proved unexpectedly successful.

The consortium of local authorities school building projects (CLASP)* formed in 1957 on the initiative of the Nottinghamshire local education authority (in the first instance to deal with mining subsidence) has been followed by other similar groups covering building, furniture and equipment. These developments have led to substantial lowering of costs and much greater speed in designing and erecting buildings without loss of individuality or freedom to experiment. Local authorities are building schools today for approximately the same amount of money as in 1949 despite a rise in prices of over 65 per cent. Building in the independent sector of education has rarely been as good either,

* See Glossary.

generally speaking, in design, or in price and speed. Even the governors and managers of grant-aided voluntary church schools have not until recently built as well or as economically as the local authorities, but they too are now joining the consortia. For the independent schools also to avail themselves of the facilities of these local authority consortia could be of great advantage to them, but few independent schools have the opportunity to indulge in extensive new building.

Unlike universities, which use funds made available on revenue accounts for new buildings, local authorities meet the cost of new building on capital accounts, paying off over 60 years. Furniture and equipment for new buildings is also charged to capital and is paid off variously over fifteen, twenty or thirty years. This means that new maintained schools are usually very well equipped; wisely, because there is never the opportunity again to do so well—subsequent renewals or additions to equipment have to be met from revenue and thus have to run the gauntlet every year of pre-rates-day cutting of local education estimates. This leads to great differences in standards of amenity and equipment between new and old school buildings. In 1952 one-third of all pupils in maintained secondary schools in England and Wales were in schools built before 1902.* By 1965 the situation had so changed that one half were in new schools built since 1944. The amount of new building in the maintained system gives a big advantage now over the majority of independent schools, most of which have their main premises in old and sometimes ancient buildings.

* Ollerenshaw, K. *Old School Buildings. Education*, No. 2748, 1955.

The Educational Revolution

EXAMINATIONS AND THE CURRICULUM

We may ask whether we are getting educational value for money spent each year, increasing numbers apart. Despite the criticisms of some employers and parents, there is ample proof that, on average, standards are improving. There is evidence in the number of successes in examinations the standards of which are themselves rising (although this is far from the whole of education) and from standardized reading tests. Investigations undertaken by the Department of Education and Science over many years and the survey undertaken for the Plowden Council* show substantial improvements in reading ability for almost all children other than a small minority who have special difficulties. The number of passes in the General Certificate of Education at both ordinary and advanced levels has gone up by leaps and bounds. Subject passes at ordinary level more than doubled between 1954 and 1964 and have now reached over $1\frac{1}{4}$ million. The number of subject passes at advanced level went up from 140,000 to 216,000 in the ten years.

There are marked differences in the subjects boys and girls tend to choose. Far more boys than girls tackle mathematics and the physical sciences—something which must disturb us when we have to train teachers. In 1964 twice as many boys as girls offered mathematics at ordinary level, and between five and six times as many boys as girls offered physics. At advanced level the discrepancies are even more marked. Girls prefer the arts subjects and modern languages where they do, if anything, rather better than boys. Two out of three girls who leave school with two or more passes at

* *Progress in Reading.* Pamphlet no. 50, Department of Education and Science. London: H.M. Stationery Office, 1966.

43

advanced level have passes in arts subjects only—one in three for boys—and one in four have science subjects only—one in five for boys.

There are four boys to every three girls in first-year sixths, three to two in second-year sixths and six to one in third-year sixths. Moreover, this difference is growing wider each year. This is presumably in part because more boys than girls enter for ordinary level as under-age candidates at 15, but mainly because girls are less willing than boys to stay on at school after 17. Not surprisingly, fewer girls than boys gain advanced-level passes, those girls who do attempt advanced level take fewer subjects and, on average, girls' results are poorer than boys'. Many boys in third-year sixths are repeating advanced-level subjects to improve grades. This the girls, with usually one year less in the sixth, are blessedly unable to do, but in the scramble for university places the handicap is severe. This disparity, however, has serious effects in the recruitment of women teachers. Girls will tend to leave school at 16 and 17 partly because they are already at that age 'going steady' and are actively contemplating marriage, and partly because there have been until recently relatively few opportunities for employment that require A-level passes (but not degrees) other than the executive branch of the civil service. Even for this girls have to stay two years in the sixths and then go on for training, whereas boys with A-levels have always been able to find good jobs as student apprentices in industry or commerce at 18.

A new development in 1964 was the establishment of the Schools Council for the Curriculum and Examinations.* This took over the work of the Secondary School Examinations Council which had been set up in 1917, and it also assumed an altogether greater influence on the work in

* See Glossary.

schools than had ever been possible before for an advisory or working committee sponsored by the Department of Education and Science. During its first year at work the Schools Council produced some notable working papers,* on science for the young school leaver, on raising the school-leaving age, on English and other subjects. The Council has initiated studies on mathematics, foreign languages, the humanities and engineering science. The Council works through panels and sub-committees whose members are almost all practising teachers or teaching and research staffs of the colleges and universities. This is the first time in the history of education in England that central agencies have attempted to influence subject teaching in the classrooms. Provided this does not get out of hand and powers remain wholly advisory, nothing but good can come to maintained and independent schools alike. They can always reject the Schools Council's ideas if they wish.

The Certificate of Secondary Education is also a new development for pupils who are not likely to be successful in the GCE. CSE examinations were held for the first time in 1965, for some 60,000 candidates. The CSE is a national certificate designed to be under the direct control of the teachers and schools themselves, with external moderators. The idea is that pupils should be examined on what they have been taught, rather than be taught what they are to be examined on. This is intended to give greater freedom to teachers to develop their own schemes of work and to match syllabuses to the special interests of the pupils. The deliberate attempt to give back to teachers some of the individual control of the curriculum which, as the years pass by, seems to be continuingly eroded can only be good. Fourteen boards have

* Working Papers nos. 1 to 7, The Schools Council. London: H.M. Stationery Office, 1965–66.

been set up to administer the examination and they work under the general supervision of the Schools Council in collaboration with the National Foundation for Educational Research. There is a suggestion that eventually, when the Certificate of Secondary Education has become fully established, it may supersede the ordinary level of the General Certificate of Education, leaving advanced level mainly as a qualifying examination for advanced courses in higher education. A number of the girls' public schools are experimenting with the CSE; if GCE O-level is to disappear more schools will need to begin developing CSE courses.

The new emphasis on the education of pupils of average and less than average ability which has resulted from the recommendations in 1963 of the Newsom Committee (not to be confused with the Public Schools Commission) is also important. Sir John Newsom was chairman of the Central Advisory Council for Education (England) from 1960 to 1963 when the needs of these less able pupils between the ages of 13 and 16 were considered, and the Report* *Half our Future* is referred to by his name. This report said a good deal about making the work in the last years at school for the less able pupils outward looking, and the schools have since been energetically developing Newsom projects which link school work to service in the local community and to employment. The idea is that these projects should catch and hold the pupils' interests in a meaningful way and make possible a successful extension of general education for those who otherwise have little academic motivation and easily become bored with school and unco-operative in learning.

* *Half Our Future* (the Newsom Report). London: H.M. Stationery Office, 1963.

The Educational Revolution

YOUTH EMPLOYMENT, CAREERS ADVICE AND SCHOOL COUNSELLORS

The links between school and work and between school and further education have been given considerable attention in recent years through, in particular, the work of the Youth Employment Service which has greatly developed its careers advice for sixth-formers. Youth employment officers try to interview all pupils, together with their parents, at least once in their penultimate school year and again before they leave school for employment. This gives an opportunity for youngsters to orientate their last year at school toward the kind of work they think that they would like to take up and avoids many frustrations. The youth employment officers prefer to work closely with school staffs and almost all the larger maintained secondary schools have a member of their teaching staff specially designated as a careers' master or mistress with responsibility (but not always enough time) for guiding pupils in their choice of school subjects, relating this to future careers or jobs. The whole structure of employment and of opportunities for gaining qualifications in further education is changing so radically, so quickly and so continually that no one who is concentrating on teaching in a school can hope to keep up with all new developments and give really sound advice without the help of specially qualified people from outside the schools. The variety of work available and the extent of specialization at work is increasing and the Industrial Training Act is bringing new requirements so that careers' advice needs to become correspondingly more professional. Good though the work of the Youth Employment Service is, it needs to be greatly extended and many more young men and women of calibre need to be recruited to it and given special training.

47

The Educational Revolution

Many girls from maintained and other schools take on casual jobs during the holidays and on Saturday mornings—mostly in shops, restaurants and hotels. Some do regular paper rounds and other delivery jobs before or after school. So long as there is moderation, this can be useful social training as well as a source of pocket money, and it does provide something of an introduction to the world of work. Girls at direct grant and public day schools usually have too much homework in preparation for examinations to keep up such work regularly, although they sometimes work all day Saturday in city stores. During term this is usually actively discouraged by the schools because of the considerable strain it entails.

The task of entering sixth-formers for universities and colleges and of giving them sound advice about which college and course to choose is usually the responsibility in grammar schools of the headmaster or headmistress. Indeed, the number of university entrants and awards a school can achieve each year is often as much the result of the skill of the head in gauging correctly where each contestant should aim, and of the energy which the head is prepared to give to the whole business of university and college entrance, as of the intrinsic merits of the would-be students. This is one of the reasons why the public schools, in particular the boys' public schools, have had until recently a distinct advantage over most state schools—the heads of the public schools mostly have an intimate knowledge of the Oxford and Cambridge colleges and 'know the ropes'. Conversely, some heads of grammar schools of all kinds have tended to be shamefully ignorant of what has been going on in higher education outside the universities, with serious losses for technology and for many of their school-leavers who might have found greater fulfilment in newly developed technological and social science courses than in studying for traditional university degrees. As comprehensive schools develop, careers' advice will become of greatly increased importance; girls' schools in particular have tended to neglect the development of good careers advice services.

School counsellors are also now becoming a popular innovation mostly in the larger comprehensive schools. The Americans have always had counsellors in their high schools, but the traditional attitude in this country has been that the teachers themselves should have full pastoral responsibility for the pupils they teach. In this country we have not wished to seem to separate the process of teaching from that of looking after the child's general well-being, and there has been and still is a good deal of resistance to the idea of having counsellors. In the public boarding schools housemasters and housemistresses fulfil this role.

However, as schools become larger, time-tables more complex, youngsters more sophisticated, families less settled, and paid work outside school during term more commonplace, school counsellors may be natural additions to both day and boarding school staffs. Already they are proving their worth in some schools and they are sufficiently numerous now to have formed themselves into a professional association.

FINDING THE TEACHERS

Of all the problems of the past ten years, finding the teachers has proved by far the most intractable. Teacher training colleges—now called colleges of education—have had to be extended, new colleges built, more students with good qualifications recruited, and, even more difficult, well-qualified and experienced staffs found. College lecturers have largely had to be drawn from the schools themselves, thus

D

depriving the schools of experience which could ill be spared.

Since 1956, local authorities have been allotted each year a quota of full-time teachers based on the number of children in their schools. This is to make sure that no area has more than a fair share of teachers who are thus encouraged to take up posts where need is greatest. Before the introduction of this quota system some popular areas could recruit all the teachers they could pay for while other areas were left denuded. The quota system is generally regarded as having worked well; it does not apply to direct grant or independent schools, and there is some antagonism on these grounds from those who want to see these schools integrated with the state system. Part-time teachers and full-time married women returners during their first two years of service do not count against the quota. Although the number of full-time teachers is expected to continue to increase marginally in the next year, all local authorities heard in January 1967 that their quota is to be reduced and classes, already large, will be slightly larger. This is partly to ensure that the less attractive areas are not further handicapped by the failure to find enough teachers to keep pace with the rising numbers of pupils in the schools. There has, however, been considerable success overall in increasing the number of teachers. The number of full-time teachers in schools increased by over 20 per cent in ten years to nearly 300,000 in 1965, with, in addition, over 36,000 part-time teachers, most of whom were married women. Over 60,000 more teachers are needed to get rid of oversize classes—a gap which may take another fifteen years to overcome even if the raising of the school leaving age in 1970–71 is disregarded.

Efforts to attract more men into teaching have shown considerable success. In 1956 four out of ten teachers in training were men; in 1965, four out of nine. The two-year general course was superseded by a compulsory three-year course in 1959. Various devices for increasing the load on colleges, for example four-term years, unpopular though some of these are with both staff and students, are helping substantially to increase the output of trained teachers through a more intensive use of accommodation—that is, if the students are not so put off that all enthusiasm for teaching wanes and they give up; a really serious threat. Although most married women teachers leave the schools when they start a family, the increasing capacity of the colleges is creating a large reserve of women teachers, many of whom, it is hoped, will return to teaching when home circumstances permit. The break in service varies from a few months to many years and some teachers, of course, never come back to the schools. At present, of every hundred women who enter the colleges, only forty-seven are in the schools after three years' service, and after six years only thirty.* Only time will tell how many will return.

In addition to the increase in the number of trained teachers coming from the colleges of education each year, the increase in the number of new university graduates is helping to swell the teaching force, although insufficiently. Education is rapacious; the universities and the colleges themselves have also to be staffed. Sometimes we seem to be winning, but forecasts about teacher supply are notoriously unreliable. There are warnings now of tough years in the immediate future; some 9,000 extra teachers were expected to be in the schools in 1967–68, but the new estimates show that this increase will reach only 7,000. Where the lost 2,000 are is not known for certain but some may have drifted into

* 9th Report of the National Advisory Council for the Supply of Teachers. London: H.M. Stationery Office, 1965; and the Plowden Report.

51

secretarial jobs or have decided to marry earlier than fore-
casters predicted. Crowded conditions in the schools do
nothing to stiffen the resolve of the waverers to carry on; if
girls going to the colleges of education have no serious intention of making a career in teaching, and if university
graduates turn their backs on school teaching as a career the
prospects will indeed be bleak. One half of all women
graduates go into teaching as it is; it is difficult to see how we
are to persuade a still higher proportion to teach now that
nearly all professions are open to them. Although in the early
days the girls' public schools were the greatest contributors to
the teaching profession, some of the public boarding schools
in the years between the wars failed to convince enough girls
of the value of taking up teaching. There are signs that
recently this has been changing and that more public school
girls are entering the colleges of education.

In the past few years a great deal of new thinking has gone
into the teaching of mathematics and science. There have
been intensive courses for serving teachers, and syllabuses
and methods of teaching have been revolutionized. Parents
making casual visits to primary schools may sometimes feel
that no learning is taking place—and certainly small children
are no longer drilled in multiplication tables or made to sit
at fixed desks every day doing money sums. There is, however, a fundamental weakness which may take many years
to eradicate: over 50 per cent of women and until recently
over 25 per cent of men going into the colleges of education
have not reached the standard of an ordinary-level pass in the
General Certificate of Education in mathematics. This has
been so since at least 1957 and the situation is deteriorating.*
Some of these students openly say that they chose to train for
infant schools for no other reason than that they disliked

* See Plowden Report.

mathematics themselves at school or consider themselves to be no good at it. Evidence of competence in mathematics is normally an entrance requirement for the colleges of education. None the less many young teachers have a frighteningly slight understanding of the mathematics they must teach when they first go into the schools to face a class. Most of them in the primary schools will be class teachers responsible for mathematics—we may well be alarmed about the effect on their pupils. All the new methods and interesting practical work in the world cannot compensate in the schools for teachers' inadequate knowledge. As the majority of teachers in junior schools and nearly all teachers in infant schools are women, and as the foundations of mathematical understanding must be laid at the primary stage (to an extent that is not so imperative for history or modern languages, for example), the situation is serious when students go out to the schools for teaching practice, and even become qualified, without having demonstrated any real understanding of the subject that they will be required to teach. This is equally true of every subject, but mathematics is particularly vulnerable and the effects of muddled teaching of mathematics at the early stages is especially hard to remedy.

In-service courses for teachers nowadays abound and good work is done at them, but much of this is largely remedial; the onus lies with the girls' secondary schools. They must not allow girls who are contemplating teaching to drop mathematics and could well run special short courses, maybe in sixth forms, in which girls could be taken through the elements of primary school mathematics from an adult point of view. The colleges could perhaps curtail some of the time spent on child psychology and art in favour of the content and methods of mathematics teaching.

The development of four-year courses and degree courses

will do much to raise the status of the colleges and to make teacher training more attractive. These degrees in education may be under the auspices of the university to whose area the college belongs or, in the future, may be degrees of the Council for National Academic Awards (which will be discussed later) the college itself administering the course and the examinations. Experimental part-time training courses for teachers already exist. Another new development is the siting of 'departments of education' in a few leading technical colleges, which will undertake three-year general training courses mainly directed toward teaching in primary schools. The four long-established technical teachers' training colleges deal mostly with mature students on one-year or sandwich courses, training teachers for further education colleges and for technical subjects in secondary schools.

The first day training colleges for mature students were started some years ago in Manchester and in Leeds. They have sent out into the schools over the past fifteen years a steady flow of teachers, mostly women, who for one reason or another did not want or were not able to go from school to residential colleges at the usual age. All colleges now accept day students and a few were established to provide day training for school leavers. Accommodation for this and other expansion has often been provided by converting abandoned schools and other property.

All this adds up to a many-angled attempt to find potential teachers. This unremitting effort must surely have its reward some time. In the long run perhaps salary scales alone will settle how many men take up teaching, but salaries are not the predominant issue for women.* Physical conditions in some schools, impressions of authoritarian attitudes and

* Kelsall, R. K., *Women and Teaching*. London: H.M. Stationery Office, 1963.

feelings about low social status however mistaken may tend to deter some people from teaching. But secretaries earn far less than teachers, have longer hours and shorter holidays; and salaries in most medical ancillary work are pitiful. Teaching can be a really exciting job full of creative opportunity, but somehow either we have failed to convey this to some girls in sixth forms or we are damping their enthusiasm in the colleges or during their first terms as new teachers in the schools. We need to examine carefully the underlying reasons why we lose so many teachers after they have begun training. Marriage is an obvious cause, but not the only one. Plainly many girls leaving school see the colleges of education as a second best to the universities. If GCE advanced-level passes are not in high grades this may be as good a way as any to have three years of student life on grant. It gives a chance to get away from home and gain some independence, whereas for most other forms of non-university training they will be expected to live at home. There is no equitable reason why girls should be denied the opportunity of higher education in the colleges of education using them however blatantly as liberal arts colleges, for this compensates for the disproportion between the numbers of men and women in the universities. There can be no better training for future wives and mothers than that given in preparation for teaching young children and there is always a chance that they may acquire a taste for teaching and make this a real career. This, however, does not solve the teacher shortage.

We could do more to hold these students, or at least not to go out of our way to put them off. If they have over-long distances to travel each day from inadequate college lodgings to far-away schools for teaching practice, sheer physical tiredness can make them dislike the work. The answer here would surely be to arrange for good lodgings near the school for the practice year—anyway during the week. Students are sometimes used as substitute teachers and are too often given tough jobs in understaffed schools. Throwing newly qualified teachers in at the deep end, giving them big classes or placing them in schools in difficult areas, may have been a good sink-or-swim initiation in the old days when trained teachers walked the streets unemployed. Today this does not work; young women teachers climb into one of the many lifeboats, take up secretarial work or any other occupation where employers are clamouring for good staff and fill the gap, if any, between training and marriage in work other than teaching.

Teacher centres now being set up by local authorities will be a most valuable factor in helping young teachers over their first two or three critical years. If we are to have the teaching force we need, as much energy and more must be put into the welfare side of caring for newcomers to the profession as we have been putting into recruitment to training and into persuasion for those who have left to return.

EXPANSION OF FURTHER EDUCATION

Growth in education after school outside the universities has, if anything, been even more dramatic than that in the schools. Numbers of students in full-time further education in Great Britain have risen to over 175,000 and the number in all forms of further education has increased by a half since 1955 to over three million. The White Paper, *Technical Education*, of 1956* set in trend a new and vigorous expansion

* *Technical Education* (Cmd. 9703). London: H.M. Stationery Office, 1956.

based on a rationalized system of colleges grouped into four categories: colleges of advanced technology with wide and near-national recruitment; designated regional colleges; area colleges; and local colleges. Within this framework progress has been spectacular and the ten colleges of advanced technology have all now become autonomous universities.

The British system of further education forms an effective link between school and work and plays a role as an educational gap-filler unmatched in any other country in the world. It provides an alternative route to the professions and is unique in the manner in which it gives a second chance, or even provides a first choice in its own right, for those people who for one reason or another do not follow the conventional pathway to professional qualification through the schools to universities, seeking full-time employment only after graduation. Moreover, the close links which the colleges have with industry and commerce can bring a special stimulus to students who see immediate aims and purpose in their work. When practical experience in real situations is combined with theoretical study many students make a most favourable response.

Further education is a natural growth from the tough days of the last century and the beginning of this century when boys left school at twelve and worked their way up to the top of their professions by the hard way of night school, particularly in engineering and the manufacturing and construction industries. The tradition of the people with the best academic brains tending to choose white-collar jobs dies hard. As opportunities in full-time higher education increase and more of the ablest pupils in schools proceed to the universities, the technological industries have tended to lose some of the best brains in the country. There is still an in-built resistance, largely caused by ignorance, in sixth forms and in the older universities to courses with a technological slant and to the technical colleges, despite a growing realization of the national loss this brings.

The number of students under the age of 18 following full-time courses in colleges of further education increased three-fold in the ten years 1954 to 1964 from 30,000 to 90,000. Increases in part-time day students particularly of girls have been disappointing over the past few years, partly because of the new pattern of staying on at school. In 1965 only 7·4 per cent of girls in employment aged under 18 were given day release to attend further education classes. Even so the number of boys and girls under 18 in part-time courses rose from 175,000 in 1954 to over 281,000 in 1965. Now that the effects of the Industrial Training Act of 1964 are just beginning to be felt the increases may again become really big. The Act will affect girls as well as boys and gradually all young workers under 18 will have to attend courses in education and training.

Part-time courses leading to National Certificates, the City and Guilds of London Institute examinations and other qualifications have been revised and rationalized and new courses for techniques and craft workers introduced. The idea has been to provide a structure of vocational courses* leading to qualifications at all levels which will guide students through from success to success, rather than allow them to aim too high and court heavy failure rates. Failure is still too frequent, but there have been serious attempts to match the theoretical content of courses to the real rather than supposed needs of the career aimed at.

Further education between the ages of 16 and 18 has been of particular importance in filling the time for many young

* *Better Opportunities in Technical Education* (Cmd. 1254). London: H.M. Stationery Office, 1961.

people between leaving school and serious adult wage earning or going on to advanced level work at college or university. In the United States a different pattern obtains. Youngsters have to be either 18 or high school graduates to qualify for entry to college; if they leave school at 16 or 17 there is no way save through military service to bridge the gap and still get back successfully into full-time education. These early leavers are dubbed drop-outs and only recently has any serious attempt been made (and even that only here and there and in the cities) to provide 'work-study' courses for them in which work is combined with part-time study. In the United States there is not the same tradition of evening study on which to build a firm structure of part-time day-release courses.

OVERLAPPING COURSES

Antagonism has long existed in some areas between the local colleges of further education and neighbouring secondary schools trying to build up extended courses. Girls in particular who begin to feel bored with school are attracted by the idea of leaving and attending a local college full time instead. While the colleges and schools offer overlapping courses for the 16 to 18 age groups the conflict will remain. Competition between schools and colleges need not in itself be bad so long as it does not lead to waste of resources in buildings, equipment and teaching staffs. If the schools, whether maintained or independent, want to hold their pupils they will need to adopt new ideas and treat senior pupils more as college students. There are even experiments with bringing strictly vocational courses and examinations into the schools in order to hold pupils in new types of sixth forms. Except in rural areas or in other special circumstances this could be regarded as a retrograde step. The youngster's gain is what matters and the numbers in full-time education, not the prestige of this or that institution and how big a share of the 16 to 18 age group the schools can hang on to compared with the colleges.

If local authorities, to help their comprehensive schools to build up sixth forms or for any other reason, withdraw full-time courses for under 18's in their local colleges, as is threatened in some parts of the country, the loss for girls could be great. There are eleven girls to every eight boys aged 16 in full-time courses in colleges of further education. The girls often go to the further education colleges because they can have a secretarial training there, but some are in fact doing the same GCE courses as they could have had at school. Girls being what they are, if they are told that these courses are available only at school they probably will not bother at all. The sad truth is that whenever a choice lies with girls themselves, as it must after they reach the school-leaving age, almost any administrative decision made to increase educational efficiency and give a seemingly better return for money always seems to work against their best interests. This perhaps is because a girl's education, unlike a boy's, does not lend itself to being measured as an investment in trained manpower. We never know for how long and at what levels a girl once educated and trained will work. But the paid work that women do, even in summation, is only a small part of their contribution to society.

The expansion of further education at the higher levels has been even more significant than the increase in non-advanced courses. The number of students over the age of 18 following full-time and sandwich advanced courses in colleges other than universities increased fourfold between

1954 and 1964 from 25,000 to 100,000. The opportunity is now available through the Council for National Academic Awards which was established by Royal Charter in 1964 for students to gain degrees at all levels—ordinary, honours and postgraduate—fully comparable with those granted by the universities in some of the colleges maintained by local authorities. The Council for National Academic Awards superseded the National Council for Technological Awards which granted its first Diploma in Technology in 1958.CNAA degrees may be gained in any approved academic discipline whether in science or technology, the arts or social sciences. Courses must be approved by the Council and approval is difficult to obtain. In October 1966, 249 women were reading for CNAA courses in science and technology and 98 for courses in arts and social studies, compared with 5,907 and 835 men respectively. How many of these women had attended independent schools is not known. Stringent conditions have been set for the quality of the proposed courses, the qualifications of the teaching staffs, the form of government and internal management of the colleges and the standards of their research, library and general amenities. A new White Paper* now proposes the creation of a limited number of polytechnics from among the leading colleges of further education which remain with the local authorities now that the colleges of advanced technology have become autonomous universities. The development of designated polytechnics will have significant effects on the growth of the Council for National Academic Awards degrees which is already surpassing all expectations.

The original National Council for Technological Awards and its sucessor the Council for National Academic Awards

* *A Plan for Polytechnics* (Cmd. 3006). London: H.M. Stationery Office, 1966.

have pioneered and developed within the British system of education the pattern of integrated or sandwich courses which combine industrial or commercial training with academic study to a high level. The sandwich can be thick, thin or 'end-on'. A typical thick sandwich consists of two years in college, one year in industry or commerce followed by a final year in college. End-on courses are usually made up of alternating periods of six months in college and six in industry or commerce over four years. Sandwich courses are a logical and sound educational development of the old hard-way route of part-time evening study, which used to drag over many years of grinding self-denial and which gave rise to appalling failure rates. The growth of scientific knowledge and the imperative need for a greater amount of time given to theoretical study in order to attain full technological competence within industry made this development essential.

The Council for National Academic Awards has also announced its intention to approve courses leading to the degree of Bachelor of Education, a new B.Ed. A majority of the colleges of education have already made arrangements with the universities for degree courses, but the Council for National Academic Awards will offer an alternative for some colleges and may make a significant contribution to expanding the opportunities for teachers in training to study for degrees.

The Council for National Academic Awards is well placed, too, if and when the time may seem ripe, to encourage the development of part-time degrees in a variety of disciplines in colleges which have previously established full-time CNAA degree courses. Even more advantageous, for married women in particular, would be if the Council found itself able to encourage suitable colleges to develop degree courses which could be transferable; for example, if two years at one college followed by a course of two years at another, with or without a break in between, could lead to a full degree. Some universities do give partial exemptions for uncompleted degree courses at other universities. What the demand would be for a credit system of this kind is uncertain, but on the face of it this seems a most attractive proposition for married women, many of whom find that they have to move house from one part of the country to another because of husbands' changes of job. The difficulties would be immense but the possibility is there and the Council for National Academic Awards may have exactly the right kind of flexibility to explore this.

Women have not yet taken to technology in more than tiny numbers. In advanced courses leading to recognized qualifications in engineering, technology and applied science men outnumber women by 120 to 1 in the colleges. This seems ridiculous when in Russia one-third of all qualified engineers are women. In all advanced courses in further education colleges men outnumber women by nearly nine to one. None the less, these colleges have much to offer to women. They can be more flexible than other education institutions about hours, timetables, terms, and in the nature and content of the courses they devise. The girls' schools need to become more aware of the variety of opportunities available for girls and for mature women in the revolutionized colleges of further education. To ignore this is to ignore the greatest potential advance for women of this century. Oddly enough, the girls' independent schools seem to be more alive than other schools to opportunities in further education: over 50 per cent of all girls who left independent schools recognized as efficient in 1964 went into full-time further education other than teacher training, compared with 25 per cent of girls who left direct grant grammar schools, 19 per cent who left maintained grammar schools, 7 per cent who left technical schools, 7·5 per cent who left modern schools and 3·6 per cent who left comprehensive schools.

THE UNIVERSITIES

Alongside the development in the local authority schools and colleges there has been similar dramatic growth in the universities. The Robbins Report on Higher Education,* with its voluminous appendices, is a bible of information and statistics. Although some of its major recommendations have not been adopted, the report has provided a framework for expansion. Oxford University subsequently held its own public inquiry under the chairmanship of Lord Franks and published a major report† in 1966.

The universities fall into eight main categories: Oxford and Cambridge; the four ancient Scottish universities; the University of London; the older civic universities; the University of Wales; the younger civic universities which grew up under the tutelage of the University of London; Keele which was sponsored jointly by the Universities of Oxford, Manchester and Birmingham, and the other 'new universities' created since the war and given full degree-granting powers from the start; and now the ten universities which have grown from the colleges of advanced technology. The form which university status is to take for the Welsh

* *Higher Education* (the Robbins Report) (Cmdn. 2154). London: H.M. Stationery Office, 1963.
† *University of Oxford. Report of Commission of Inquiry* (the Franks Report). Oxford: The Clarendon Press, 1966.

College of Advanced Technology is still under discussion, but along with the other nine it is already on the grant list of the University Grants Committee. Where sandwich and integrated courses were a feature of the colleges of advanced technology they will, it is to be hoped, be retained and strengthened in these new universities; these courses have provided invaluable links with industry which have developed over the past ten years as the result of much hard work.

By the end of 1967 there will be in all thirty-three universities in England, one and possibly two in Wales, eight in Scotland and Queen's University, Belfast. In addition the University of Manchester Institute of Science and Technology and St David's College, Lampeter, receive Treasury grants through the University Grants Committee. A second university at Coleraine in Northern Ireland, the new University of Ulster, plans to admit its first students in October 1968. Plans for a new technological university or institute in the north-east are still in abeyance. Trinity College, Dublin, as well as Queen's University, Belfast, have long been attractive alternatives for some public school girls who fail to gain places at Oxford or Cambridge, and Coleraine may also in due course have its own pull for girls who have attended boarding school in Great Britain, just as now many public school girls go to universities in France, Germany and Switzerland.

The number of full-time students in universities and colleges receiving grants from the University Grants Committee (not counting those in the then colleges of advanced technology) has increased from just over 50,000 in 1938–39 to 80,602 in 1953–54 and to nearly 140,000 in 1964–65.*

* *Returns from Universities and University Colleges in receipt of Exchequer Grant* (Cmd. 3106). London: H.M. Stationery Office, 1966.

The Educational Revolution

The predictions of the Robbins Report have already been overtaken. Between one quarter and one third of the full-time students in 1964–65 were women. There has been a small but steady increase in the percentage of women over the past five years. In 1964, 8,800 girls, that is 2·7 per cent of the age group of girls, and 19,200 boys, that is 5·6 per cent of the age group of boys, left school to go to the universities. Over a thousand of the girls came from recognized independent schools and 1,240 from direct grant schools. Oxford and Cambridge, which are the largest after the University of London, have increased relatively modestly; Oxford now has 9,450 undergraduates. One in eight of the girls going to university from recognized independent schools or from direct grant schools went to Oxford or Cambridge, compared with one in twenty of those going to university from maintained grammar schools. The University of Manchester with its Institute of Science and Technology had 8,637 full-time students in 1964–65. Other universities, some of them with spacious sites and some with fairly plentiful lodging facilities, have as much as doubled in size over the past ten years. That the new universities should have got off to such a flying start in the face of this great expansion in the established universities is remarkable and a great tribute to their sponsors.

Girls from the public schools have tended not to go to the older civic universities, except to the professional schools within these universities. In medicine and in law there have always been a trickle of public school girls to the universities of Liverpool, Manchester and Leeds and probably to the other universities in this group. This is understandable because the traditional aim of the girls' public schools is to steer girls into the professions.

The new universities are proving popular choices for

women. This is partly because the numbers of women who can be accommodated at Oxford and Cambridge are severely restricted, and the competition to gain places is hardly worth the effort except for girls of clearly exceptional ability. Many really able girls who earlier would have tried for Oxford or Cambridge now prefer to put down other universities as their first choice and avoid disappointment, the new universities and the new courses and unusual combinations of subjects which they are offering attract these school leavers now. Some of the new universities are committed to giving girls a fixed number of places irrespective of their competitive ranking in entrance qualifications, at least in certain disciplines, as has happened for many years in most university schools of medicine. Because of girls' relatively low attainments in the physical sciences and mathematics the tendency has been for the universities to admit girls who may be less highly placed in these subjects than some men who are rejected.

Those new universities which are within easy reach of London have a special appeal. London, with its theatres, art exhibitions, concerts and new films, and its recent reputation as the swinging city, has a great pull, especially for bright and lively girls who have good brains but do not see themselves devoting their lives to academic study. Brighton is only one hour's journey by train from the centre of London and students at the new University of Sussex can get up to town for a theatre with minimum difficulty. Sussex University has proved so attractive to women that there has to be discriminatory selection in the arts subjects to prevent the student population from becoming predominantly female. In consequence, the academic ability of women students at Sussex is said to be on average above that of the men. The men place the older universities higher by comparison in their order of preference. York and Lancaster similarly are attracting academically well-qualified women applicants. The question is how long this is likely to last. The large numbers of girls' admissions have always been in arts and social sciences—and it is in these fields that the new universities have so far been able to make their impact in the early years. Provision for arts and social sciences both in accommodation and equipment is relatively inexpensive; to build and maintain laboratories takes both time and money. Perhaps women, after all, are born to be pioneers in this kind of educational development and find special satisfaction in being in at the birth of new institutions; or perhaps it is the new buildings and lovely surroundings which appeal to them.

A higher percentage of women than men students are in colleges or halls of residence and a lower percentage in lodgings. The policy in English and Welsh universities, other than the University of London, has always been for students if possible to be in colleges or halls of residence. In Scotland the tradition is different; in 1964–65, 45 per cent of men and 42 per cent of women in universities in Scotland lived at home. This is a policy that English universities may have to think about more seriously before too long if university provision is to continue to increase and yet the cost to be kept within bounds. Meanwhile, the habit of 'week-ending' among students is growing; commuter trains between Liverpool, Manchester, Leeds and Sheffield, for example, are packed on Friday afternoons and early on Monday mornings with students criss-crossing between home and university whether they reside in halls of residence or not. The urge to go home depends on many factors beside travelling distance; these are usually social, and often have to do with the momentary state of relationship with, and location of, the current favoured partner of the opposite sex. This contrasts strongly with the rules which governed the patterns of behaviour before the war in, for example, the women's colleges at Oxford and Cambridge where then, as now, 'keeping nights' was rigorously enforced. Only in most exceptional circumstances was any undergraduate allowed to be away from college overnight during the eight weeks of full term.

The preference of girls for arts degree courses is as marked in universities as in the further education colleges. More than three out of five women choose the arts or social studies, compared with one out of three men. Only 480 women in 1964–65 were reading applied science in universities, compared with nearly 20,000 men. The cumulative reasons of which we know—the girls' apparent lack of mathematical talent in comparison with that of boys, the shortage of good teachers of mathematics and the physical sciences in the girls' schools, lack of mechanical skill and the rest—do not add up to an adequate excuse for the magnitude of this discrepancy which does not exist on this scale in any other highly industrialized country in the world.

Unfortunately the returns from the universities, although now separating social studies from other arts courses, do not show languages separately. There is a good deal of evidence to show that this is where girls can excel. They do better than boys on average in modern languages at both ordinary and advanced levels of the GCE and they do well in advanced courses in modern languages in the further education colleges. If a girl is good at languages when she begins a degree course, she tends to go from strength to strength and outstrips the men. Schools for interpreters on the continent have the same story to tell. More information from British universities on this would be useful and, fed back to the schools, could give great encouragement to girls. Whereas girls lag in mathematics perhaps they can take a significant lead in foreign languages. Although jobs for interpreters are at present scarce the contribution to the nation of having more people competent in a variety of foreign languages would be considerable, particularly now that Great Britain is seriously seeking entry to the Common Market. The girl who has an additional qualification—art, for example, or a science—as well as good foreign languages will have unlimited opportunities.

Competition for places in the universities is becoming increasingly fierce. In general, competition is more intense for the arts and social sciences; the universities are probably over-provided at present in provision for science at undergraduate level. As girls are most interested in the arts subjects this weights the balance further against them. There is to be a considerable expansion in medicine; parents and public schools should be thinking about this, re-emphasizing the tradition of educating the future women doctors at a time when the nation is desperately short of medical practitioners of every kind.

University expansion is unlikely to be as fast in the next quinquennium as it has been in the past four years. There is evidence that the overall increase in student numbers will be permitted to be only small; efforts will be made to avoid any reduction in the places made available to entrants from the schools, but increases in the number of postgraduates may have to be curtailed.

As has already been mentioned, there are political pressures to establish a system of higher education parallel to the universities under the auspices of the local education authorities. Some people see this as a way of getting higher education on the cheap. If that were really the reason it might be good sense, for certainly university education for all or nearly all those capable of benefiting by it could, and maybe will, prove on present standards prohibitively expensive before many more years pass. The local authority polytechnics will be regional institutions, but mostly situated in the large cities, and most students will be able to live at home and will be expected to do so. These polytechnics will also build on a tradition of using colleges for both day-time and evening courses, and the use of buildings and equipment will be heavy. College terms are longer than those in universities and courses overflow into vacations. The development of end-on sandwich courses already described means that some polytechnics may never close except for national holidays. Detailed studies have been made recently of the use of resources in local authority colleges and new guide lines about size of classes on the various courses are being laid down. Advanced courses have to be approved by Regional Advisory Councils and by the Department of Education and Science—restrictions which universities would find intolerable, but which make for economy in provision. Government action is currently being taken to see that the colleges of education, polytechnics and, indeed, other local authority colleges shall have a greater measure of autonomy than hitherto in their form of governance and in conducting their academic affairs.

A lot of thought is now being given to ways of expanding higher education without reducing the whole higher education service almost to bankruptcy. Student loans are the obvious first suggestion. Whether they would achieve the economies hoped for or bring in extra income in real terms is not clear. They would result in no immediate new income, but would be only a promise of tax to come—incomes can be taxed by other means. For women they would be a disincentive to take up work or to return to work after marriage —no salary, no repayment—as well as being an anti-dowry, although there is said to be some tax structure which could overcome this. An obligation for qualified women to teach, for example, for at least two years before they could gain full certification and salary increases might be a better investment policy. Student loans for second degrees and postgraduate diplomas, to encourage and make these possible rather than for any money that these might bring in, are another matter and we should go all out for these forthwith. On balance, the only effective saving that can easily be envisaged is to think more in terms of home-based provision for higher education whether in the universities or the polytechnics.

THE WORK GIRLS CHOOSE

The revolution in education has been matched by changes in the work that girls choose, although tradition dies hard. The factories still claim a large proportion of school-leavers who have no examination successes—wages are relatively high for 16-year-old girls, but there are virtually no career prospects. Shops and the distributive trades also claim their share of women workers, but increasingly girls regard office work as of higher prestige even though wages may be low and, without qualifications, prospects are as dismal in an office as in a factory.

Clerical employment of one kind or another is by far the greatest attraction for girls entering employment from school at the age of 16 or 17, that is for girls with ordinary-level passes in the GCE but no advanced-level passes; hairdressing also attracts a substantial number of these girls who could aim at the sub-professions. Clerical employment can mean anything from clerking in a back-street warehouse, running messages and preparing tea, to working as a personal secretary—although only those of exceptional talent and personality can aspire to the top posts supporting men in positions of influence and power which give such a glamorous image in magazine stories. Good secretaries become indispensable treasures to their employers and many women who could become managers and top executives in their own right if they had earlier gained the required qualifications tend to remain for a working lifetime making their contribution in subsidiary posts.

There are many new careers developing from the expansion of technology; the growing computer industry provides perhaps the biggest new opening for girls who have even a trace of mathematical aptitude. Computers are now becoming essential equipment in every large industrial and commercial concern, in local and central government and in the nationalized industries. There is work here for girls at every level—as punch-card and punch-tape operators, as minders of other ancillary machines, as programmers and, at the top, as systems analysts and computer installation advisers. Here is a great new industry where opportunities are equal between men and women, provided that the women are prepared to meet the challenge. Women have the right propensities—care and attention to detail—needed for computer work and there is no special barrier of difficulty except that of unfamiliarity. A girl who starts work in a computer department and who is prepared to stay long enough to overcome initial lack of understanding will acquire the knack after six or twelve months and find the field of promotion wide open if she is prepared to remain and to continue to learn. For those with advanced-level passes or degrees in mathematics the sky is the limit in work with computers. Graduates in other disciplines can also find openings. Programmers who are already experienced can often find 'take-home work' to tide them over a year or two while looking after young children, but it is usually necessary to keep in close touch with developments. New techniques and new computer languages are being adopted all the time, and even a couple of years of total absence can be difficult to make up.

Teaching and nursing are by far the most favoured careers other than secretarial work for girls who have GCE qualifications. Together they account for three-quarters of all women at work in professional, technical and administrative posts. The list in order of popularity after these two professions runs thus: medical auxiliaries (with only about a tenth of the numbers in nursing), laboratory assistants, civil service executives, social welfare workers, draughtswomen, librarians, secretaries and registrars of companies, medical practitioners, authors and journalists, painters and sculptors, scientists, local authority officers. After this we come down to very small numbers of a thousand or less—trade union officials, civil service administrators, surveyors, architects, and town planners, mathematicians and economists, dentists, lawyers, qualified accountants, and, fewest of all, engineers. There are fewer than 500 qualified women engineers.

Women doctors have an important part to play in preventive medicine, in public health services, in caring for young children, adolescents and women. They nearly always marry before or soon after qualifying and they usually seem to marry doctors. For this reason they tend not to be available for long for other than part-time employment. They none the less give a large amount of unrecorded help to their husbands and, to put their value at its lowest, they form an indispensable reserve in any civil defence provisions. In the hospitals now we depend on immigrant doctors. The medical schools are being expanded, as they had to be if the Health

The Educational Revolution

Service is not to collapse, and women may be able to claim their share of available places if there is to be a proper balance and reserve of qualified women doctors. Dentistry is particularly suitable for women because it can be practised on a part-time basis. There are many different occupations in the professions supplementary to medicine which appeal to women—pharmacy, radiography, physiotherapy, orthoptics, speech therapy, dental hygiene, laboratory technology, medical illustration (both photographic and graphic art), and medical social workers.

Art has always been popular with girls and the colleges of art attract full-time women students for art education and training at every level. Advanced courses in fine art, in graphic design, in three-dimensional design, in textiles and fashion and in photography lead to good opportunities for women with artistic and practical talent. Art education for those with the right gifts and pertinacity can combine much of what is best in general education, in creative activity and in artistic and emotional satisfaction and, at the same time, opens up a wide variety of possible careers, many compatible with the ties of women's married life. Music does not fall into the same category, partly because the field of employment is more limited: only the exceptionally talented can make the grade as top performers in an intensely competitive field, but more teachers of music are desperately needed.

Sound broadcasting, television and journalism—all three also tough competitive fields—give equal opportunity for men and women. The pace is hot and remuneration chancy: only the best succeed. But they offer the attraction of free-lance work, and women of initiative and wit who have a talent for projecting their personalities while expressing the viewpoint of other less articulate women can achieve great renown through newspaper writing and through broadcasting. The test lies in keeping up high standards week after week and year after year so that respect and influence become thoroughly established.

About one-third of both boys and girls leaving recognized independent schools go straight to employment. Most of these boys seek careers in recognized professions or white-collar jobs selling furniture or cars or insurance, or they become gentlemen-farmers; but girls from public schools will enter the same range of jobs as girls from maintained secondary schools. Public school boys rarely if ever become craft apprentices or enter unskilled work, but it is not thought at all odd for a public school girl to become a 'beautician', or florist, kennelmaid, stable girl or stewardess. Perhaps this is because girls with reasonably assured incomes and almost certain marriage ahead are more genuinely free than are boys to choose what they want to do regardless of pay or long-term prospects.

The importance of teaching and other work in the education service including school and college librarianship is emphasized throughout this book and need not be discussed separately here, but nursing requires almost the same number of women recruits each year as the teaching profession. Great changes have recently taken place in the education and training of nurses, with training opportunities at several different levels. To become a State Enrolled Nurse good school records are sufficient: to embark on training as a State Registered Nurse GCE passes are required. Salaries are improving, regulations are being altered to be more humane and to match modern ideas; training techniques and teaching methods are being revised. There are now opportunities for girls to read for degrees which lead to nursing at the highest levels as matrons and sister tutors.

Librarianship is popular for girls with GCE passes at

either ordinary or advanced level who do not go on to study for a degree. Credit for A-levels is also now given in other branches of local government service, including the Police Service, in a new trainee grade authorized in 1966; but except in work involving computers and in librarianship not many girls go into the local government service at 18.

No discussion of employment for women is complete without mention of facilities for working part time. Half-time and part-time work has always been a feature of industries which have been dependent on unskilled women—textiles and the potteries being the outstanding examples. Only recently with shortages in some of the professions becoming acute—notably in nursing and teaching—has part-time work for qualified women been greatly extended. The hospitals had to come to terms with part-time and half-shift working if the wards were to remain open: the schools, reluctantly at first, had to follow suit. Most of the girls' public schools in particular are dependent on part-time married women teachers and they find that this works well. In a secondary school, where most teaching at best is by specialists in the various subjects, part-time teachers can make an invaluable contribution without too much complication of timetables. Married women coming to a school part time can add their own richness of experience and freshness of approach: their horizons are not blurred by the minutiae of school life and their outside contacts are appreciated by the pupils. Unfortunately, the availability of part-time work other than in nursing and teaching seems to vary inversely with the level of education and with the length of training involved. Part-time work in industry and commerce has inherent limitations: management at high levels requires long hours and full-time presence and attention. Moreover, if a woman gives up her employment for ten or fifteen years while bringing up a young family she lacks the experience that men gain as they work through to the top of their professions.

Training for mature students, retraining, part-time training, 'packaged year' higher education and training are important developments for women. The opportunities are there and are growing: it remains for women to learn about them and, if they have the desire and the will, to take advantage of them. In the past most girls from the leading grammar and public schools whose families could afford to support them did not expect to remain in full-time employment after marriage. They would not be idle, but would give their time after the needs of home and family were met to voluntary work. Nowadays most voluntary work requires qualifications: the days of amateur 'good works' have largely passed. Whatever their prospects girls cannot afford today to neglect to avail themselves of the opportunities there are for training for some specific occupation or career. To have qualifications and at least some experience in employment before marriage is a valuable insurance for a woman against the tragedy of early widowhood, divorce or other catastrophe, and, more important, it gives confidence and enables her to make a full contribution to the community according to her own choosing and circumstances in whichever of the many roles she may be called upon to play—as wife and mother, as paid or voluntary worker outside the home, as citizen and elector in a democratic society.

CHAPTER THREE

The Movement Toward Comprehensive Schools

Confusion about what comprehensive education means and about what constitutes a comprehensive system of secondary education is widespread. Few people who are not professionally engaged in education understand what all the talk of reorganization on comprehensive lines is about; even teachers seem sometimes not to have appreciated its implications. Governors of schools, parents and the general public cannot be expected to have followed and understood all the plans and counter-plans put forward by local authorities, so that only when a school in which they have a particular personal interest is threatened with radical change of status or function do they become alarmed. By then not only are they probably too late to save whatever they feel it is important to save, but as they are insufficiently well informed the arguments they use are often less effective than they might be.

SELECTION

One of the most common misconceptions is about selection itself. Selective secondary education, contrary to what is sometimes thought, was not a consequence of the 1944 Education Act. It had developed progressively from the very beginning with the foundation of the early grammar schools in the fourteenth, fifteenth and sixteenth centuries. The 1870 Act made provision for compulsory elementary education with the undisguised purpose of having a literate working class, the education going little beyond the 'three r's'—reading, writing and arithmetic. The underlying assumption was that the middle and upper classes would find something better privately. After the 1902 Education Act, when secondary education on the rates became permissive, selection was written into the regulations. The Supplementary Regulations for Secondary Schools, 1907, laid down that '. . . . a proportion of school places shall be open without payment of fee to scholars from Public Elementary Schools who apply for admission, subject to the applicants passing an entrance test of attainments and proficiency such as can be approved by the Board . . .'. The Hadow Report* of 1926 and the Spens Report† ten years later both saw selection as natural and right. Grammar, technical, modern and some 'multilateral' schools were clearly defined, approved and operating before the outbreak of the second world war. The doubts about the suitability of grammar school education for all children of secondary school age were clearly stated in the Spens Report: 'Perhaps the most striking feature of the secondary schools . . . is their marked disinclination to deviate to any considerable extent from the main lines of the traditional grammar school curriculum. . . . The present difficulties . . . have arisen largely out of the confusion which began about 1904 between a type of secondary education appropriate to

* *Education of the Adolescent* (the Hadow Report). London: H.M. Stationery Office, 1926.
† *Secondary Education with Special Reference to Grammar Schools and Technical High Schools* (the Spens Report). London: H.M. Stationery Office, 1938.

the needs of boys and girls between the ages of 11/12 and 16/17 and the traditional academic course orientated towards the universities.' Again, the Norwood Report* of 1941 shows how the educational thinking of the time was set on selection: 'The evolution of education has in fact thrown up certain groups, each of which can and should be treated in a way appropriate to itself', and a White Paper of 1943, *Education Reconstruction*, which foreshadowed the 1944 Act said: 'After eleven, secondary education, of diversified types but of equal standing, will be provided for all children.' This White Paper, but not the 1944 Act itself, spoke of grammar, technical and modern schools. The words of the Act were: 'all children should receive, without payment of fees, a secondary education suited to their ages, aptitudes and abilities from the age of eleven'—the famous three a's.

Secondary modern education was to be the great new step forward, free of examinations and especially geared to meet the needs of some 70 to 75 per cent of children who were deemed not to be suited to extended examination-orientated schooling. The secondary modern schools were the brain child of educationists, not of parents. Nomenclature in education has always been overlapping and often misleading. Before the war, secondary education had been used synonymously with grammar school education and the public's interpretation in 1944 of the new promised land of secondary education for all was of grammar school education for all. In the event, secondary modern schools as a whole barely got off the ground. Under inspired heads, in new and well-equipped if overcrowded buildings, the best of them became show pieces, and parents whose children had not gained places at the selective schools, grudgingly at first and then

* *Curriculum and Examinations in Secondary Schools* (the Norwood Report). London: H.M. Stationery Office, 1941.

with enthusiasm, praised what these new schools were doing for them. But too many of the so-called modern schools were little other than the old elementary schools in the same old buildings, modern only in name and with nothing to indicate their new status except perhaps a classroom converted and re-equipped for domestic science or typewriting. Not until 1958* was the Government of the day able to allocate money specifically for replacing and renovating the older secondary school buildings. Long before the building work then authorized was completed the attack on selection as such had gathered force and the cause of the modern school was lost.

Intelligence tests, developed much earlier by psychologists as measures of ability, were seized on for the purposes of selection at 11 years of age on the theory, which is becoming discredited, that intelligence is largely innate and that an intelligence test at 11 was a reliable indicator of a child's potential, unbiased by the quality of the primary education the child had experienced, home background, environment or other important characteristics such as persistence and powers of concentration.

This naïve view of the efficacy of the intelligence tests, and indeed of the innateness of intelligence, gradually began to lose ground. More refined tests for 11-year-olds were developed which took account of attainment in the basic skills of reading and writing and of competence in number work and in problem arithmetic. This, in turn, had a backlash in the primary schools, inhibiting, for example, new developments in the teaching of mathematics, and putting an undue emphasis on speed rather than on gaining understanding of underlying principles. Local education authorities developed

* *Secondary Education for All. A New Drive* (Cmd. 604). London: H.M. Stationery Office, 1958.

different techniques for combining the assessments of pupils' abilities given by the primary school heads with the results of the tests and in putting right, by reference to adjudicating panels of teachers, the more immediately obvious errors in the placement of individual children. Some local education authorities devised means of allocating pupils to different types of secondary schools without resorting to eleven-plus examinations. This meant that the primary school heads had to make selection judgements. Many of them preferred not to have to take this responsibility, and indeed there is a point of view held by some elected members of education committees and by some parents that heads' assessments are even more prone to bias than the discredited tests.

All the refinements could not obscure from parents the fact of selection. A process which before the war had been known as 'taking the scholarship', with pride in success for those who were chosen for the grammar schools, became 'failing the eleven-plus', with acute disappointment, at least at first, for a majority of the parents of the 75 per cent or so of children who were not successful in gaining places in grammar or technical schools. Eleven years of age is too young for selection which may seem to set a ceiling to ultimate achievement, especially when, undeniably, selection processes themselves tend to condition the child's subsequent progress. But selection at some stage there has to be. Had the age of transfer from primary to secondary schools been postponed for all children until twelve-plus, as is now recommended in the Plowden Report, the popular feeling against selection for secondary education might have been by that much less strong.

Equal educational opportunity has long been the aim of all liberal-minded people. The ideal of the examination-free modern school failed because the way to the top in almost every career nowadays lies through examination qualifications. The professions are demanding ever more stringent entrance requirements for the courses leading to their examinations; technicians and craft workers need certificates if they are to rise to the more highly paid grades. Until the modern schools began to develop GCE courses they were doomed to lack of prestige. Gradually they introduced examination streams, and, as more of their pupils stayed on for a full fifth year, they were able to offer ordinary-level courses in several GCE subjects. Many of the modern schools which are now being absorbed into comprehensive systems had already strong fifth forms: a few had sixth forms as well. Modern schools could never have been expected to have a full range of sixth-form subjects, but pupils could transfer, and many have been transferring, to sixth forms of other secondary schools which have selective or comprehensive entries.

Meanwhile, the idea of providing all types of secondary education within one comprehensive school had been growing. Whether or not there is selection within the comprehensive school is an internal matter, but the argument is that this does not carry the 'stigma' of selection. Selection to different types of secondary schools, even if genuinely of equal status, had become unacceptable to a large section of the public. The maintained grammar schools (and the direct grant schools) had given the abler working-class children real opportunity; but the less able still seemed to be left in a second tier. Middle-class parents who could afford fees had the choice not available to the less well off of sending their children, if they failed the eleven-plus, to private schools offering a grammar-school type education. Before the modern schools have had a chance to grow to maturity and show their real worth, we have therefore followed our usual practice in this country of rushing into something new and not fully tested which it is hoped will do the total job better, hunting the illusory snark of universal equality. Unfortunately we never seem to have enough money to give new ideas a proper start or time to mature; circumstances seem to force us to take on too much with too little.

Politics play a big part in education policy making; this is inescapable in a democracy under a party political system, for education today is both big business and big money—public money, over £1,500 million a year of it. General and local elections are the only method of testing the will of the people. On the single issue of abolishing the eleven-plus, if a nation-wide plebiscite were feasible, although the poll might be low because at any one time only a limited number of people have a special interest in schools, few can doubt that there would be an overwhelming majority vote in favour of abolition. A promise to get rid of the eleven-plus has proved a sure vote winner. The present Government is wholly committed to the abolition of all selection by ability or aptitude to different kinds of schools, though many Government supporters have serious reservations. Opposition opinion is less clear cut, and would continue to allow modified selection by ability as educationally necessary, particularly when teachers and resources are hard to come by.

The organization of secondary education without selection and the consequences of doing this are difficult to explain. We have very little hard evidence to draw on. Although there is a steadily growing number of comprehensive schools in existence and the success of many of them is unquestioned, there are still, in 1967, no local education authorities in England and Wales other than Anglesey where all secondary education is in comprehensive schools. For individual comprehensive schools to be a success is to be expected: whether an all-comprehensive system of state education can succeed equally is another matter.

The Movement toward Comprehensive Schools

However, the very success of the 1944 Education Act and its central tenet of secondary education for all has brought public opinion to an increasing dislike of barriers within the state system whether social or intellectual. Greater affluence; the gradual elimination of the grosser forms of poverty, at least on the surface; full employment and the increase of leisure; the steady flow of youngsters from working-class backgrounds (not as many as had been hoped but significant in effect) who, despite all handicaps, have succeeded in fighting their way through to the universities; the new emphasis on the education of the less able children—all these factors and many others of like force have created a situation wherein sympathy toward the comprehensive idea was bound to spread. Comprehensive education is a symbol of egalitarianism. When we all know that we are equal and when there is genuine equal opportunity, then we can afford to be as different as we wish and dispense according to whim with conformity. Meanwhile, a majority of the British public have come to think of selection for secondary education as 'unfair'. This is strong condemnation; for better or worse, selection at eleven is on the way out. The bipartite and tripartite systems of grammar, technical and modern schools have played a critical part in the evolution of post-war secondary education. Without selection over these past twenty years and the concentration of able pupils and scarce graduate staff, the phenomenal growth of sixth-form work leading to the universities might never have been possible. We may still find that we are not yet ready to dispense with selection altogether without seriously damaging academic standards in some parts of the country.

The Movement toward Comprehensive Schools

COMPREHENSIVE SCHOOL PATTERNS

Children's aptitudes and abilities vary widely. To meet the needs at the secondary stage of each individual child different types of secondary education are needed. To provide these a system of different secondary schools was a natural first development. In 1947 only one child in every eighteen stayed on at school beyond 16 years of age. To gather together into selective schools the ablest children most likely to stay on was as sensible a policy then as was the provision of a carefully thought out four-year secondary school course for the majority who would almost certainly leave at the earliest permissible opportunity whatever school they were in. Immediately after the war a comprehensive school recruiting from a full cross-section of the ability range was thought to have to be, and indeed had to be, very large indeed by English standards—over 2,000 pupils—if it could hope to develop viable sixth forms. Although London and Coventry went ahead with building these big schools, most local education authorities did not favour the idea, partly because they wanted to have maintained grammar schools of their own and partly because of their uneasiness about very large schools and the lack of big enough sites on which to build them. Ten years elapsed before two-tier comprehensive schools were developed in Leicestershire; this deliberately divided secondary education into two stages and made possible a form of comprehensive education in schools of 400 or 500 pupils.

In fulfilment of pre-election promises, the Labour Government, after nine months in office, issued the famous Circular 10/65 in July 1965 on the organization of secondary education. The Circular began, 'It is the Government's declared objective to end selection at eleven-plus and to eliminate separation in secondary education'. It went on to outline ways of achieving this objective and requested local education authorities to submit plans for their areas on these lines within a year. These plans were to be drawn up on the assumption that the age of transfer to secondary education would remain at eleven, although by then most people in the know were already well aware that the Plowden Report was almost certain to recommend a later age of transfer. Some people were greatly disappointed that Lady Plowden's committee had not found themselves able to give an interim judgement in advance of the full report on this specific issue. Early in 1964 Mr Quintin Hogg, the then Secretary of State for Education and Science, had guided an Education Act through Parliament allowing for the establishment of a relatively small number of schools catering for children of ages straddling the division at eleven years old between primary and secondary schools. When local education authorities began to submit plans under Circular 10/65, these powers were extended by the new Secretary of State for Education, Mr Anthony Crosland, to permit the establishment of 'middle schools' whenever a case is made out for them as a means of reorganizing on comprehensive lines.

The six main comprehensive systems proposed in the Circular were:

(i) The orthodox comprehensive school with an age range of 11 to 18 years.

(ii) A two-tier system whereby all pupils transfer at 11 to a junior comprehensive school and all go on at 13 or 14 to a senior comprehensive school.

(iii) A two-tier system under which all pupils on leaving primary school transfer to a junior comprehensive

school, but at the age of 13 or 14 some pupils move on
to a senior school while the remainder stay on in the
same school.

(iv) A two-tier system in which all pupils on leaving
primary school transfer to a junior comprehensive
school. At the age of 13 or 14 all pupils have a choice
between a senior school catering for those who expect
to stay at school well beyond the compulsory leaving
age, and a senior school catering for those who do not.

(v) Comprehensive schools with an age range of 11 to 16
combined with sixth-form colleges for pupils over 16.

(vi) A system of middle schools which straddle the
primary–secondary age ranges. Under this system
pupils transfer from a primary school at the age of
8 or 9 to a comprehensive school with an age range of
8 to 12 or 9 to 13. From this middle school they move
on to a comprehensive school with an age range of
12 or 13 to 18.

The first proposal is that most favoured when buildings
can be designed from scratch. The idea that an all-through
11-to-18 comprehensive school has to be very large indeed
in order to produce viable sixth forms is now being modified.
The bigger age groups since the war, the tendency for
pupils to stay on longer at school, the growth of sixth forms
and the plans to raise the school-leaving age to 16 in 1970–71
have moved the centre of gravity of secondary education
toward a higher age. However, account must be taken of
regional differences and of the areas within regions from
which pupils to a particular school will be recruited. If we
take national average figures, a simple calculation from the
Statistics of Education 1965, using the 13-year age groups
and sixth-form numbers in grammar schools and in all

maintained schools, we find that, theoretically, if ability were evenly distributed among all schools all organized on strictly comprehensive lines, the number of 13-year-olds in a comprehensive school still needs to be four times as great as in an average grammar school today which recruits from the top 20 per cent of the ability range if it is to produce sixths of the same size. In the cities, grammar schools have usually aimed at an intake of 90 or 120 pupils a year—that is, they are mostly schools of 'three-form' or 'four-form' entries* with about 700 or 800 pupils in total. But a twelve-form entry comprehensive school, leading to a total of about 2,000 pupils in all, is nowadays considered too big a unit as well as an impractical proposition in cities with sites of only limited size available. In a good area, and in the South-East where youngsters tend to stay on longer at school than, for example, in the North-East, comprehensive schools taking about 240 pupils a year, that is, eight-form entries, and with a total size when fully developed of about 1,300 pupils can be expected on present averages to have a hundred pupils in the sixth. In poor areas, the logic seems to show that the schools still need to be much larger than this to give the abler pupils a real choice of subjects at sixth-form level. So also do schools for girls only, as fewer girls than boys stay on beyond 16.

A number of all-through comprehensive schools are being given sixth-form units which will contain common rooms for pupils (perhaps we should forthwith call them all students?), facilities for them to do their own entertaining, reading rooms, study corners and so on. The Department of Education and Science is itself co-operating in designing and building prototype sixth-form units in collaboration with some local education authorities.

Few if any of the plans now being submitted to the

* See Glossary.

The Movement toward Comprehensive Schools

Department of Education and Science by local education authorities are for schemes which depend entirely on all-through 11-to-18 schools each in one building. For most authorities this is ruled out, at least in the short term, because they have to make use of existing buildings which are not big enough to become all-through comprehensive schools in isolation.

THE SPLIT SCHOOL

A new variation of these three two-tier systems outlined in the Circular has since developed. This is the 'split school'—a combination of two or more separate existing schools called one school. This gives in theory an orthodox 11-to-18 comprehensive school, but in more than one building and with the pupils moving on from one building to another at the end of their second, third or fourth year as the case may be. This arrangement has some of the advantages of the two-tier systems described in the Circular in that pupils are never in a very large school unit; and some of the advantages of the all-through 11-to-18 school in that the pupils remain together throughout their secondary school life. The staff belong to one school even if operating in different buildings and the curriculum can be a continuous whole. The split school also gives a convenient solution to the problem of reorganizing secondary education on comprehensive lines in existing buildings.

The split schools have disadvantages too. Pupils will normally not move between buildings in the course of a school term or year and so they will not have the combined facilities of the whole school for their use at any stage. Either the staff stay almost all the time in one component of the school or another, in which case the school is in effect two or more different schools, or there must be a good deal of to-ing and fro-ing of members of staff between distant buildings. Accelerated promotion from one building to another could be a form of hidden selection, but to have no possibility of accelerated promotion could seriously handicap the ablest pupils. The quality of staff in all sections of the school needs to be good, but there is high probability that the best qualified staff will want to spend all or most of their time in the building that contains senior pupils. The opportunities for truancy of pupils, which has been reaching horrifying proportions in some maintained secondary schools in recent years, could be hugely magnified in a split school. If the pupils of a year group, say at fourteen, have to be divided between different sections of the school because of the precise size of the component buildings, genuine 'setting' across an age group according to ability in different subjects would become virtually impossible.

TWO-TIER SYSTEMS

Proposal (ii) of the Circular has the difficulty that if pupils attending several junior comprehensive schools are free to choose between two or more senior comprehensive schools, curricula need to be carefully co-ordinated between all the schools involved. Moreover, the lower tier 11-to-13 or 11-to-14 schools covering so short an age range might come to be regarded as in-and-out 'transit camp' schools and be unattractive to teachers. This is partly true for proposals (iii) and (iv), and these also contain an element of selectiveness whether on recommendations relating to ability to profit by extended school education or by parental decisions which might restrict a child to a minimum length of school course.

Support for proposal (v) of the Circular, the system of a number of 11-to-16 comprehensive schools feeding into a few 'sixth-form colleges' has not been as great as might have been expected. The opposition is cogent. Grammar school heads feel especially strongly that pupils of good academic ability aiming at universities must be put firmly on the road by at least 13 and that they need five years of teaching by graduate staff with sixth-form experience. If pupils meet with strict academic disciplines first at 16 then they are likely to be one or two years behind the performance expected in the leading grammar schools today. This would tend to bring British education more in line with American education at the very time when America is introducing fundamental reforms to try to bring their system up to the educational standards of ours, measured by the attainments of the abler youngsters of 16 to 18 in our present grammar schools. The best qualified graduate staff usually want some share of sixth-form teaching and would tend not to be content to teach only in an 11-to-16 school. Heads of 11-to-16 schools might also feel great frustration if they were for ever denied the opportunity to develop post-ordinary-level GCE work. None the less, the shortage of graduate staff in some subjects may force a concentration of sixth forms. One of the consequences of creating all-comprehensive systems everywhere may well be that sixth form colleges become inevitable.

All the devices for two-tier systems have a distinct disadvantage in the education of girls. A recurrent theme in this book is the difficulty of holding a girl's interest in education throughout adolescence. Any break of school between 14 and 16 can cause a loss of interest, although in special circumstances it may give a new start. Few headmistresses, and they are the people who can be expected to know best,

favour the idea of two-tier systems of secondary education for
girls.

THE MIDDLE SCHOOL

The sixth of the suggestions in the Circular for organizing
on comprehensive lines is to create a primary school or 'first
school' from 5 to 8 or 9, a 'middle school' from 8 or 9 to
12 or 13, followed by a senior school. This pattern has already
been planned in certain parts of the West Riding. The advantage would seem fairly plain and the educational argument for a first school followed by a middle school has been
clearly made out in great detail in the Plowden Report.
Unfortunately even here there is confusion. The West
Riding scheme will plump for nine and thirteen as the ages
of transfer, but the Plowden Report says eight and twelve,
although the precise recommendation is rumoured to have
been taken only after long debate. In a sense these are only
marginal differences of principle. The basic idea is that there
should be three stages of schooling, first school, middle
school, and senior or high school, that is a 4–4–5 or 3–4–6
structure for the thirteen years of schooling from 5 to 18,
instead of two years in an infant school, four years in a junior
school and seven years from 11 to 18 in a secondary school.

Educationally, there are real advantages in the middle
school arrangement provided (and this is a vital proviso) that
the standards of teaching and of equipment and amenities in
the middle school are equivalent to those required for
children of 10 to 13 in the best schools now. The best primary
school education today is very good, as the Plowden Report
so well relates, but, as the report also points out, there are
still grave shortcomings in many areas. Experiments with
different kinds of comprehensive organization are welcome,

but only when they are carefully planned. Although there was a great chance for establishing middle schools as a method of getting rid of the eleven-plus and of raising the school-leaving age by building for an extra year of education in the younger age groups rather than for an extra final year, this opportunity now seems to be past. Almost everywhere the spate of new building for both primary and secondary education on a different pattern will preclude any further change to a middle school arrangement for a long time to come.

CROSS-SETTING

In any comprehensive school various devices for breaking down the large numbers of pupils into reasonably small groups can be introduced—vertical divisions into 'houses'; horizontal year-groups, with tutors moving up through the school with each age group and so providing continuity in pastoral care; junior, middle and senior departments and so on. No two schools need be alike in internal structure. There may or may not be streaming according to ability; the popular idea now is to delay streaming as long as possible and certainly to have as much flexibility between streams as can be managed in the first two years. Cross-setting, that is, multiple grouping according to individual abilities in different subjects, is the method preferred although this is not good pastorally if carried too far. The ablest pupils tend to be good at most if not all subjects and cross-setting may in practice be little more than a slightly refined form of streaming. If pupils are genuinely unstreamed for a group of subjects throughout their first two or three years then they may have a sense of not being completely divided from one another according to fortuitous ability.

Cross-setting for, say, science requires that there are at least as many laboratories and as many teachers of science all available in one building during the same lesson period as there are science sets in one year group. In practice this is rarely so even in a large school, and in a split school cross-setting will be by that much more difficult to arrange. Whenever there is a substantial amount of cross-setting, time-tabling becomes very complicated indeed and great care is needed to ensure that some pupils do not get left out from some subjects altogether—not from choice, even if choice about dropping some key subjects ought to be easily per-mitted, but purely for reasons of expedience. There are educational advantages in having a big school; the larger staff makes possible a greater variety of subjects and special interests and the school can more easily overcome casual vacancies, for example, in modern language staff. Facilities for every kind of craft and practical work can be made available: art and music can be taken to very high standards.

Any system has disadvantages as well as advantages, and every system will have its casualties. Selection gives more homogeneity in ability groups and greater opportunity to concentrate staff with special abilities to teach these groups. To have no selection by ability to different kinds of secondary education may postpone the unpleasant task of differentiat-ing between pupils on their past and present performance, but this differentiation has to be made at some stage and, indeed, is being made consciously or unconsciously by every teacher in every lesson all through a child's school life. Not to admit the existence of special talents and, when they are revealed, not to see that they are developed to the full is the grossest neglect both of the child and of the potential wealth of the nation. We all know of children in primary schools who are bored and become lazy because they can do the work too easily. Children need the excitement of learning in an atmosphere of challenge. The problem is to reconcile the ideal of developing each individual child's mental, physical and spiritual abilities to the full in a situation where compromise is inescapable. Most of us would agree that for the ablest children to make some sacrifice is right if we can be assured that this is genuinely for the good of the majority. No one, however, has made any objective measure or even an acceptable guess at what the net gain for the majority is in having in their midst a small number of very able children, especially if the latter are not able to develop to their full capacity because of lack of stimulation of enough youngsters of equal calibre, and lack of enough well-qualified specialist staff.

THE NEIGHBOURHOOD EFFECT

The type of organization which finds popular favour at any one stage in the history of a nation's education system depends on the predominant aim of the moment. Just now the aim of the theorists would appear to be to obtain a true social and intellectual mix in every school. Except in a rural area, where one school will serve a whole community, this is probably impossible to achieve. In the cities, if there is to be no selection by ability, recruitment of pupils to the different schools can indeed be by parental choice in the first instance, but after a time the 'neighbourhood effect' would appear to be almost unavoidable and is already appearing here. American experience is that people will move house frequently, even mortgaging themselves to the hilt, in order to live within the catchment area of the best school available. Good schools become better, the bad schools cannot improve themselves; a hierarchy develops and this can become an influence at least as divisive socially as any system which selects by ability.

Parents here will be able to say which school they would like best for their children, naming, say, three schools in order of preference and the choice will then be met 'as far as is practicable'. This complies with the principles of the 1944 Act and is the most that can be expected within a state system of comprehensive education. Special reasons, in particular denominational religious education, or if a brother or sister is already attending a desired school or a parent attended that school, will be taken into account. But once a popular school has filled all its places, allocations will be made on the only remaining valid basis, that of residence. Priority will be given to those children who live nearest to the school.

Wise parents therefore will go to any length to try to live as near as possible to a comprehensive school with a good reputation—either choosing a house carefully in the first instance or removing at the first opportunity if they consider that the school serving their area is not good enough. This favours those parents who can afford to be owner-occupiers and who are free to move house.

The theory is that new housing policies will ensure that social segregation into distinctive residential neighbourhoods with a clear income group structure is eliminated. Common observations show that this aspiration seldom squares with reality. Even when planning committees deliberately encourage mixed housing development, private developers are slow to come forward with schemes for building houses for sale in the middle of large local authority estates. Industrialized building may also tend to encourage large housing schemes catering for people with similar income groups.

Eventually more mixed development, the aim of nearly all liberal-minded people, is sure to come, but this will be slow and will certainly lag behind the present wholesale switch to comprehensive schools.

There is evidence in the Plowden Report which would seem to show that the brightest children living in poor surroundings and being taught with a group of low attainment and bad home backgrounds tend to suffer most from attending school in their own immediate neighbourhood. These are just the children who have most to gain academically by a system which allows them to escape from the environment of their home to a school elsewhere, which happens in a selective system.

One way of lessening the bad effects of recruitment in natural catchment areas, which too often in cities are one-income-group communities, is to draw artificial boundaries for different schools in an attempt to create a greater social mix. This is being done in America to hasten integration between white and Negro pupils. It is difficult to operate, almost impossible to enforce and universally unpopular. So far no local education authority has ventured to introduce this device to achieve social mixing in schools here, although immigrant children in some towns are transported to school from one area to another to avoid too large a concentration of foreign-language difficulties in some schools to the detriment of the education of indigenous children.

The former London County Council went some way toward lessening the neighbourhood effect by controlling the intellectual intake into its comprehensive schools on the basis of intelligence tests given in the last year of primary education. No individual comprehensive school was permitted to recruit solely from those children with the highest intelligence quotients. The city of Norwich has proposed a plan for 'going comprehensive' now in this way. This does, however, smack of gerrymandering and is seriously suspect from some educational as well as social points of view. For example, just how are the pupils from within any one specified intelligence range, say, above an 'intelligence quotient' of 125, to be chosen for a favoured school—by lot, or first come first served or by what method?

THE ABLEST PUPILS

The sheer momentum of expansion and the growing desire of parents for their children to have an extended education is certain to increase dramatically the number of pupils staying on at school beyond 16. None of the official statistical predictions given earlier take account of any possible effects raising the school-leaving age may have on parents' desire to keep their children in school even longer voluntarily merely to gain an available advantage. Growth at the top of the secondary schools is certain to be great, independently of any reorganization. As there can be no scientific control system, no one will ever be able to assess whether this growth would have been greater or not as great if reorganization had not taken place.

There must be, however, serious misgiving about the possible effect of universal reorganization on comprehensive lines on standards of academic achievement of the ablest pupils at a time when well-qualified graduate staff are so scarce. A calculation on averages here proves interesting: we can take as a specific and clear-cut example the number of teachers in schools with first or second class honours degrees in mathematics. In 1965 there were 2,170 in all maintained secondary schools in England and Wales and

283 in direct grant grammar schools. A breakdown of the figures shows that two out of three maintained grammar schools, one out of two technical and comprehensive schools and only one out of every 37 secondary modern schools might expect now to have one member of staff with a good honours degree in mathematics. Every direct grant school could on average have one, and two out of three have two. If all maintained secondary schools are taken together there is one of these teachers to every 1,300 pupils; if all maintained and direct grant secondary schools are taken together the ratio is 1 to 1,200 pupils which is not significantly different. Under a fully comprehensive system everywhere there could be on average one, but not more than one, member of staff with a good honours degree in mathematics in every school of between 1,000 and 1,500 pupils whether direct grant grammar schools were absorbed or not. There is an argument that it is better for every child of secondary school age to be in a school which has a well-qualified graduate mathematician on the staff than that these teachers should work in smaller schools with selected entries and some secondary schools have no mathematician on the staff. As all pupils cannot actually be taught by this one member of staff there is something to be said for ensuring that at least the head of the mathematics side is well qualified. The same sort of situation, of course, holds for graduates in other subjects particularly physics, chemistry and classics.

This, on the face of it, may be an argument for universal comprehensive education. However, teachers are not pawns to be distributed according to formulae; if they are pushed around too much, many will leave the profession altogether. And the argument is too facile; anyone who has experienced the atmosphere and intellectual drive of a leading grammar school of good size will know that there is something self-sharpening about bringing together very intelligent boys or girls in reasonable numbers and matching them with a teaching staff of proved intellectual calibre. There is a challenge and in-built stimulus which cannot and does not come about in a more mixed grouping. Possibly the pupils at the bottom of the intellectual ladder in a high-powered grammar school may find themselves left behind and suffer as a result, but this is often exaggerated. We should not ignore the experience of America and Russia, two great industrialized countries which have had universal comprehensive education from the beginning. Special schools for the top 2 or 5 per cent of the ability range are now considered to be essential as an antidote to their comprehensive systems, and are being established even in the Golden State of California. The ablest pupils have been shown to need special attention, just as in every advanced country this is provided for pupils of very low ability. Both in Russia and in the United States fully comprehensive systems have had to be modified to bring together exceptionally able pupils. Here we have looked after the top 20 per cent of the ability range in our grammar schools. A random distribution of pupils between fully comprehensive schools might well lead to a situation in which some other system would have to be considered, for example, special schools in which the top 2 or 5 per cent of pupils with exceptional academic ability could be educated together from at least the age of thirteen. If this happens then we may find that if we destroy selective schools we may have to re-create them.

THE STAFF

There will be good and less good comprehensive schools, just as there are good and less good schools of every type now. The quality of a school depends on the quality of the staff, not on the recruitment of pupils, although parental attitudes are all-important and schools in an established community are likely to have more interested parents than are schools which serve mainly itinerant populations. As in any organization or group activity, standards in a school are set and achieved through the head. A good headmaster or headmistress, given free rein to run a school as nearly as possibly autonomously, can make a success of the task even in unfavourable circumstances. But there is not an unlimited number of men and women with the almost superhuman qualities needed to be head of a large comprehensive school. Some brilliant schoolmasters are natural grammar school masters with no affinity with or sympathy for the less able child. Some headmistresses find their *métier* in relatively small schools and do inspired work with girls from difficult homes—and do not, and would not, wish to attempt the same task within or as head of a large comprehensive school. One of the great losses of going all-comprehensive could be the fall-out of headmistresses who as a group are among our finest educationists. A school is a growing organism and time is required for it to show good results. Twenty years were required for municipal grammar schools to reach the high status recently attained. Some of them are now fully equal in standards to some of the direct grant grammar schools of much longer tradition. The insistent desire of many parents for their children to do well at school will prove a big asset in building up the new comprehensive schools, but the greater the upheaval of change now, the longer it will be before reorganized schools can settle to a new forward drive. Where transition is smooth and gradual and the disturbance of teachers kept to a minimum progress need not be noticeably hindered. The risk is in too abrupt change, too violent re-dispositions of teachers into different schools and buildings, and too precipitate changes for the children. Comprehensive reorganization could in some areas cause a crisis of confidence both among teachers and, just as importantly, among parents. If so, this is bound to harm education, at least temporarily.

There is no panacea for educational ills in reorganization as such and to think so is to mislead a public which has no alternative but to believe what the pundits say until they are proved wrong, and by that time the children are grown up and another generation tries out its own new version of old ideas. We would do well to concentrate not on organization but on teachers, to take a hard look at the qualifications of the teachers we have and are likely to have—and then to fit the schools to the teachers and the pupils. We know now a good deal about the pupils—the Crowther,* Newsom and Plowden Reports have done a fine job of increasing our understanding of children in school. We know next to nothing in the same way about teachers, nor have we any objective and down-to-earth study of conditions under which they teach best, of how many teachers have the qualities that will make good heads of departments, or of how many have the administrative potential which will make them suitable candidates for headships of large comprehensive schools. Courses have recently been established for training in the organization and management of schools. The problems thrown up by large schools catering for pupils with a wide

* *15 to 18* (The Crowther Report). London: H.M. Stationery Office, 1959.

range of ability and interests and by unfamiliar types of school are of great complexity. In California teachers are not allowed to become principals of a senior high school unless they have taken a special post-experience degree at Master level in educational administration. And here we are, asked to plunge into an all-comprehensive system when many heads of the new schools have little relevant experience, some of whom are frankly sceptical of the whole theory of comprehensive education. On top of all this we are raising the school-leaving age—a reform which has everything to commend it if circumstances are right and which is anyway perhaps best not postponed. The direct grant and independent schools, standing on the brink and wondering if and at what point they are likely to be pulled into the mêlée, can hardly be blamed if they regard the situation with some dismay.

Unfortunately we are largely in the dark about which is the best way to organize a comprehensive system. We are having to make do with buildings designed for an entirely different system and so inevitably are fitting plans to buildings; when we do have the opportunity to build a school purposely for comprehensive education, we argue without real knowledge about what is the best size. Only after Circular 10/65 was issued was any full scale research initiated into the relative merits of different kinds of comprehensive systems, and there have not yet been any published results of this research which must necessarily be spread over several years.

Comprehensive education and comprehensive schools in theory can seem to be the only alternative to eleven-plus or thirteen-plus selection. A movement toward more comprehensive education was natural. We might have arrived at the same largely non-selective result less traumatically if we had worked upwards by age. Primary schools are all of them comprehensive in entry. We may be extending primary education to 12, and some local education authorities are establishing middle schools to 13. From there comprehensive education to 15 or 16 possibly with some exceptions would be a logical development. But this is not to be and the price may prove high. We know that some comprehensive schools and schemes work well, but it will take many years for them to match in academic achievement the work of the best grammar schools today. Meanwhile, if we destroy schools of undisputed worth, built up over twenty, fifty, a hundred years into institutions of unimpeachably good repute, we shall have only ourselves to blame if standards fall.

CHAPTER FOUR

The Direct Grant and Voluntary Schools

VOLUNTARY SCHOOLS

Circular 10/65 on the organization of secondary education was concerned above all with county schools—that is, schools which are wholly under the control of local education authorities—but it contained a strong request that local education committees should also include wherever possible the maintained voluntary schools in their areas in their plans for comprehensive reorganization and that they should open discussions with direct grant schools with a view to their integration within local schemes. The nomenclature is confusing and the regulations governing voluntary and direct grant schools are complex.

There are 229 Church of England, 485 Roman Catholic, and 253 other voluntary aided, controlled or special agreement* schools in England and Wales which are maintained by local education authorities. Table II shows the number of secondary schools in England and Wales by status and denomination and the number of pupils in them in the years 1960 and 1965. There has been no significant change in the number of schools or pupils of secondary school age in Church of England and other non-Catholic schools; the number of Roman Catholic secondary schools has increased by 41 per cent from 345 to 485, and the number of

* Alexander, Sir William and Barraclough, F., *County and Voluntary Schools*. London: Counties and Education Press. 3rd edition, 1939.

The Direct Grant and Voluntary Schools

TABLE II

The number of secondary schools in England and Wales by status and denomination and the number of pupils in them in the years 1960 and 1965

Status and Denomination	1960 Secondary Schools		1965 Secondary Schools	
	Schools	Pupils	Schools	Pupils
County Schools	4,984	2,390,483	4,896	2,416,892
Church of England				
Aided	139	43,642	117	40,294
Controlled	83	26,329	77	27,201
Special Agreement	25	9,667	35	13,102
Not determined	2	690	—	—
Total	249	80,328	229,	80,597
Roman Catholic				
Aided	254	90,713	360	139,597
Controlled	1	138	4	1,308
Special Agreement	90	38,392	121	54,954
Total	345	129,243	485	195,859
Other Denominations				
Aided	93	46,538	91	46,520
Controlled	165	76,311	161	78,780
Special Agreement	1	255	1	406
Total	259	123,104	253	125,706
All Voluntary Schools				
Aided	486	180,893	568	226,411
Controlled	249	102,772	242	107,289
Special Agreement	116	48,314	157	68,462
Not determined	2	690	—	—
Total	853	332,675	967	402,162
All schools	5,081	2,723,158	5,863	2,819,054

Source: Supplied on request by Statistics Branch, Department of Education and Science.

pupils in them by 52 per cent from 129,243 to 195,859 in the five years, that is from 4·7 per cent to 6·9 per cent of the total in all maintained secondary schools.

Aided schools now recover from the central government 80 per cent of the cost of new capital building. Considerable pressure can therefore be exercised in persuading them to come into line with local and central government policies. A few of the voluntary aided schools have substantial funds from their sixteenth- and seventeenth-century foundations which can be used for scholarships or capital projects.

Only about half of the Church of England Voluntary secondary schools are aided schools; the controlled schools have less independence, and all (or almost all) their capital as well as current expenditure is met by the local education authority. Few, if any, Church of England schools restrict their entries either wholly or mainly to children of parents who are communicants of the Church and from this point of view there is little difficulty in their combining with the undenominational maintained schools in comprehensive schemes. None the less, any integration of the Church of England schools within local education authority plans for reorganization presents formidable difficulties. Progress so far, even in talks about plans, has been notably slow in some areas, although in others local agreements have fallen fairly easily into shape.

Great difficulty has arisen about the more famous aided grammar schools, especially in the London area; they have much the same tradition as the direct grant grammar schools, with fine reputations for academic achievement and long histories, and some of them would be most reluctant to abandon the selective nature of their recruitment policies. In some instances, local authorities are offering voluntary schools some of their own awkwardly small or isolated modern school buildings—presumably at the price of any outstanding debt charges—so that combined buildings can form an enlarged voluntary school big enough to accept a comprehensive entry. Other Protestant denominational secondary schools and the Jewish secondary schools, totalling 253 in all in 1965, most of them widely separated geographically, are in similar predicaments to the Church of England secondary schools. Their future at the moment hangs in the balance. Those which have selective intakes are for the most part continuing or initiating their own methods of selection one year at a time pending further discussions. All this is most unsettling for them.

The Roman Catholic schools present problems of an altogether different order of magnitude. Roman Catholic schools are overfull in many areas, particularly in towns and cities in the north-west, where in consequence recruitment to local Catholic day schools is almost entirely from Catholic families. Moreover, Catholic parents normally seek places in the Catholic schools for their children. Full integration in the sense of intermixing between Catholic and non-Catholic maintained schools does not therefore arise. The aim is therefore for Roman Catholic secondary schools themselves to form comprehensive systems which may or may not match whatever schemes the local education authorities in their area are planning to adopt. There is real difficulty here as Roman Catholic dioceses seldom coincide with local education authority boundaries. The Catholic grammar schools in particular, which recruit pupils from wide catchment areas, cannot hope to reorganize their curricula and their recruitment policies in such a way as to suit equally well the varied schemes being adopted by the several local education authorities within whose boundaries their prospective pupils live.

The Direct Grant and Voluntary Schools

Catholic schools cater for only a part of any local secondary school population. They are therefore placed much as are county schools in rural areas serving scattered communities; but in the cities they have the added handicap that the children live in densely built-up areas. There are, however, nearly 200,000 children altogether in Roman Catholic secondary schools in England and Wales and there are big concentrations in some of the larger towns and cities, particularly in Lancashire. The Catholic secondary schools are mostly relatively small, many recruiting only 30 to 60 pupils each year; few of them have an annual intake of more than 120. This means that, if they are to 'go comprehensive', either two or more separated schools will have to be linked together to form one school, or some two-tier comprehensive arrangement must be devised or they must introduce a middle school arrangement or buildings will have to be extended to form all-through 11-to-18 schools. As has been said, aided schools have to find 20 per cent of all costs for new schools and extensions to existing schools. The Roman Catholic community is already heavily in debt and has made tremendous sacrifices to meet their massive school building targets since the war; any extra expenditure specifically for reorganization on comprehensive lines would be a big extra burden. The problems of the Roman Catholic aided schools, to a greater extent than other voluntary schoools, are also inextricably bound up with the future of the direct grant schools. What solutions eventually emerge and how far the Roman Catholic and other voluntary schools will feel obliged to reorganize in ways that are unpalatable to them is as yet uncertain.

The Direct Grant and Voluntary Schools

DIRECT GRANT SCHOOLS

There are 179 direct grant grammar schools in England and Wales,* 96 of which are girls' schools and one for boys and girls. Of the girls' schools one-third are church foundations, 57 of them Roman Catholic. One in forty, that is, 2·5 per cent, of both boys and girls aged 13 in England and Wales attend direct grant schools. In the 'upper schools', that is, in schools and departments for pupils of secondary school age, there were, in 1964, 46,300 girls.

Seventy-one of the girls' direct grant schools have junior departments or 'lower schools' for children under 11 years of age, and twenty-four have boarding houses providing in all for 2,000 boarders. All the girls' schools are predominantly day schools, but five in England and three in Wales have over a hundred boarders, one of them 225. Most of the direct grant boarding schools have strong denominational or local attachment, but pupils come from widely spread geographical areas and, increasingly, from overseas. Junior departments receive no grants or other assistance from public funds.

The schools are unevenly distributed geographically. Most of the schools with boarding provision are in the counties of the south and south-west. The big schools which take only day girls cluster mainly within the cities of London, Liverpool, Manchester, Leeds and Bristol and there are more in the north than in the south. In the north these direct grant day schools fulfil something of the role played by the independent public day schools in the south, probably because, when the choice of whether or not to apply for

* *List of Direct Grant Grammar Schools in England and Wales*, List 73. London: H.M. Stationery Office, 1964.

The Direct Grant School. A memorandum prepared by the Direct Grant Committee of the Headmasters' Conference (undated).

direct grant status was originally open to them in 1928, the schools in the north served less affluent communities and were more readily prepared to accept direct grant status.

The girls' direct grant schools range in size from two with just over 200 pupils to one with over 1,000; sixty of them have between 300 and 500 pupils, and another seventeen have between 500 and 600. More than one in five of the pupils in the senior departments is in a sixth form and more than two out of three girls who leave direct grant schools go on to some form of full-time advanced study or professional training.

Direct grant schools operate under regulations revised from time to time by the Department of Education and Science. They have independent governing bodies; either one-third of the governors are nominated by local education authorities or, if the school so prefers, a majority are 'representative governors'. The schools receive a capitation grant for each pupil from the Department and a supplementary grant for each pupil in the sixth form. At present the capitation grant is £39 and the sixth-form supplement £66. The capitation grants cover roughly two-thirds of revenue expenditure, that is, about the cost of the teachers' salaries. If the schools lost the capitation grant, fees would have to go up to nearly double their present level.

Twenty-five per cent of the annual intake to the senior departments must be offered, either directly or by putting them at the disposal of local education authorities, as free places to pupils who have spent at least two years in maintained primary schools. Further places, called reserved, must in addition be offered to local education authorities for pupils suitably qualified with the proviso that the number of free and reserved places shall not, unless the governors agree otherwise, exceed one half of the total intake. In many schools the proportion of free and reserved places is more than half the total number of places. The local education authorities pay the full fees for the pupils whom they nominate. The remaining places, called residuary, are awarded to fee-payers, whose parents pay the fees on a sliding scale according to income. For parents in low income groups the balance of fees is paid to the schools by the Department of Education and Science. The governors are responsible for the broad policy of their schools, and the schools are required to reach a level of efficiency satisfactory to the Secretary of State; they may not be conducted for profit.

Almost all direct grant schools, including the schools for day pupils only, recruit from wide geographical areas which cut across local authority boundaries. They bring a valuable element of social mixing, provide for denominational religious education and, irrespective of income, give to parents of children of high academic ability a genuine choice of school. The direct grant schools which take boarders make a seemingly indispensable contribution in providing for some of the pupils whose parents apply to local education authorities for help with boarding on the grounds of 'need'.

No grants are available to direct grant schools for capital expenditure, and, generally speaking, this must be met from appeals and fund-raising activities or from endowments. Few of the girls' direct grant schools have endowments to fall back on, although some, if not most, of the Roman Catholic girls' direct grant schools belong to Catholic Orders which may have resources to meet the cost of new building. The direct grant schools are almost all old foundations with a proud heritage: they include some of the earliest and most famous day grammar schools. The criterion for admission of pupils to a direct grant grammar school is laid down by regulation as the assessment of the capacity of the pupil to profit by education in the school. No pupils may be precluded from entrance because of the inability of their parents to pay fees. Moreover, preference in admission has to be given 'to candidates considered likely to profit most by the education in the school'. As the schools given direct grant status in the first instance were from among those which had outstanding academic reputations, the words 'likely to profit most' has come almost automatically to mean for most direct grant grammar schools those candidates who do best in the schools' or local authorities' examinations at eleven. Some direct grant schools have four or more times as many applicants as available places. How they could choose their entrants with fairness other than on competitive tests and interviews is not clear.

Almost all pupils in direct grant grammar schools stay on into the sixths. In 1965, 8·7 per cent of boys and 9·7 per cent of girls still at school aged 17 were in direct grant schools. One in three of both boys and girls in 1964 leaving direct grant grammar schools went on to a university compared with one in six of the boys and one in twelve of the girls leaving maintained grammar schools. In addition more than one half of the girls who left the direct grant schools went on to some form of full-time further education or to teacher training, compared with one third from maintained grammar schools.

These differences are particularly significant for girls. There is no suggestion that the girls' direct grant schools select more severely than the boys' schools, but the differences between the success of the direct grant and the maintained girls' grammar schools is twice as great as for the boys' schools. This reinforces the argument that, as has been mentioned before, the drive engendered by a school in which all or almost all girls are expected to stay on until 17 or 18 helps to get them through the 'fall-off' period around

16 years of age. If girls' direct grant grammar schools are absorbed into comprehensive schemes the loss for girls' education could be especially serious and the pace at which we can increase the number of women going to the universities might be diminished without this root-cause being exposed.

THE FUTURE OF DIRECT GRANT SCHOOLS

The direct grant schools are under a dual threat: that of the Government which under Circular 10/65 is requesting them to consider ways of integrating with local education authorities' comprehensive plans, and that of the local authorities themselves who can at any time withdraw their agreements to take up places. If local education authorities proceed with reorganization, pressures could increase. There may be a reprieve from year to year, but where political feeling runs high this may not be allowed to go on for long. Local authorities in the cities are unlikely to be willing to pay for places on a selective basis if their own schools, all within reasonable travelling distance for all pupils, have been reorganized to eliminate all selection by ability, and if they are anxious to build up sixth forms in their new comprehensive schools in the shortest possible time. If a direct grant school is large enough to become a comprehensive school itself and if governors are willing and able to accept comprehensive entries which take no regard of ability and which fit in with local authority plans, then no doubt there will be no argument about it being allowed to continue to enjoy direct grant status. The Government's objection is to selection, not to the independence that direct grant brings. But few direct grant schools are equipped or staffed to cater for pupils covering a full range of ability. Moreover, most of them feel that they are doing their best work in their present form as selective schools.

A direct grant school would be placed in a precarious position if no places were taken up by any of its contributory local education authorities. To qualify for the capitation allowance and for the balance of the fees partially or wholly remitted to some parents, the school would then have to make good the full fees of the 25 per cent of pupils allotted free places from maintained primary schools. School governors would find difficulty in raising voluntary funds to meet this annual loss of fees other than by unduly raising the fees for the other 75 per cent of pupils. Fees may not be varied without the permission of the Department of Education and Science. The steep rise in fees necessary for this would lead to a corresponding rise in the Department's subsidy to some parents. The Department may be willing to meet this rise as an interim measure while discussions about integration take place.

For most direct grant schools, certainly for most girls' schools and many of the church schools, the burden for governors of providing, free, one-quarter of the places would be too great to be contemplated. Each school would then have to decide whether to become a fully independent school for children of parents who can afford fees (with as many free places as could be managed from endowments), or to cast aside all tradition and to come under the control of the particular local education authority within whose boundary the school stands, and thus become wholly absorbed into whatever comprehensive school system is locally proposed. Whether the local authority would then have to buy the school would depend on trust deeds—denominational schools might seek (and some already have had to seek) aided status whereby they do retain some measure of independence.

The Direct Grant and Voluntary Schools

The direct grant schools would be most reluctant to lose their valuable characteristic of accepting pupils without regard to parental income and their place as a link between the fully maintained and fully independent systems. They value the independence of their governing bodies, their freedom to select (and dismiss) pupils and staff without reference to the local authority and their freedom to manage their own finances subject to the approval from the Department of Education and Science about fees and 'costs-per-place' of new buildings. For most girls' direct grant schools full independence would almost certainly prove impossible—they have not the financial resources and, even today, parents are more loath to make financial sacrifices to educate their daughters than their sons. Only if the schools have capital resources of their own and large enough sites can they contemplate increasing their size sufficiently to become all-through comprehensive schools, and even then they have to gain permission from the Department to build. Some direct grant schools may be asked if they would be prepared to become sixth-form colleges to take pupils from maintained 11-to-16 comprehensive schools. Very few are likely to agree to this willingly, although most would probably be happy to accept pupils to the sixth forms if the resources are made available for them to build enlarged sixth-form units.

The direct grant schools that now have boarders might well consider extending their boarding provision (if they can find money) to allow two-year sixth-form residential courses for girls who are paid for by local education authorities. Selection by ability would not on this basis arise; pupils who are prepared to undertake a two-year sixth-form course after 16 are self-selected. Assisted boarding provision now for able children is ludicrously inadequate, as has been shown. The 2,000 girls who are boarders at direct grant secondary grammar schools are the only girls in the country gaining a grammar-school boarding education in schools which are being helped by subsidies in the form of capitation grants from central public funds.

The direct grant schools which are religious foundations present a particularly intractable problem. Roman Catholic direct grant grammar schools for girls in the cities tend to recruit from a wider range of ability than the non-denominational direct grant schools. Moreover, they take girls from more varied and poorer home backgrounds on average than the non-Catholic schools. The homes of some of the pupils are very poor, socially, educationally and financially. These schools seem not prepared to become sixth-form colleges or to take only the academically ablest girls. Their whole tradition is orientated toward training girls from Catholic families to become good Catholic mothers and to serve the community of Catholics and non-Catholics as teachers, nurses and social workers and in a host of other professional and semi-professional occupations. Many of the schools are attached to convents and a large number of their teaching staffs may be nuns of the convents. Moreover, many of these convents and their associated schools belong to Catholic Orders and are not under the control of diocesan hierarchies. Most of these direct grant convent schools feel that to have their girls from at least the age of 13 is essential if, in the short time before they leave school, they are to be inculcated with the right disciplines and to attain sufficiently good standards in academic and other school achievements to go on to higher education. Although some of these Catholic direct grant grammar schools recruit from a wide range of ability the problem of integrating them into all-comprehensive schemes within a local authority presents great difficulties. In some parts of the country, the Catholic direct grant schools provide for the whole of the Catholic grammar school intake of large catchment areas, and the aided schools have only non-selective entries. This makes for serious educational problems, for the least favourable way to form a comprehensive school is to join together two or more separate secondary modern schools which have no experience of sixth-form work. With no sixth-form element to begin with and few financial inducements for well-qualified staff they would find it hard to 'get off the ground'.

The direct grant schools at present hold a unique place in the British educational system. They provide a real and working link between the maintained and independent schools and they have some of the advantages of both education systems. Their future is at present most uncertain. Many parents do not appreciate how acute the situation is; some local education authorities which are reorganizing their schools on the principle of 'no selection by ability' are taking the view that to pay for places in schools which still select on ability might be interpreted as condoning a policy of selection. Where, as in Norwich, allocation to the local comprehensive schools themselves is to be on the basis of an intelligence test in order to ensure an even spread of ability, a direct grant school may more easily be able gradually to extend the range of its recruitment. Where there are to be no tests at all and no primary school heads' assessments made available to secondary schools, co-operation will be much more difficult. If the movement towards comprehensive schools continues to gather strength, the direct grant schools will almost certainly be asked to modify their selection procedures and recruit by some means not yet clear over a much wider range of ability than now. Provided that they can make some gestures of goodwill on this score they may be allowed to continue for a long time yet, even under the present Government, and meanwhile attitudes may change. Some local authorities will be glad to avail themselves of the sixth-form facilities and experience of the direct grant schools, allowing pupils to transfer to them after GCE ordinary level: others may want to hold their senior pupils in their own maintained schools.

The boarding facilities which some of the direct grant schools can offer will help them. The financial principle of direct grant is not the main target of attack. The Government shows willingness to retain a direct grant system and the valued semi-independence this gives provided that the stumbling block of selection by ability can be overcome. This is, however, a crucial feature at present of most of the direct grant schools. Governors and heads of the schools must say on what principles they wish to stand firm, while co-operating in any way which is not contrary to these principles. They can, in good faith, do no less. In the last resort they may have to make the soul-searching decision about changing their status from direct grant either to become aided or maintained schools within a local authority comprehensive system or to become independent. If they choose to become independent, they will then virtually throw in their lot with the public schools which are now being considered by the Public Schools Commission.

CHAPTER FIVE

The Girls' Public Schools Today

THE SCHOOLS

In January 1967, the Governing Bodies of Girls' Schools Association had 152 independent schools in membership; these are the schools, as is explained in the Introduction, which are defined as the girls' public schools. They fall into five groups: those which have boarders only or only very few daygirls; those which are mainly boarding schools but have between, say, 5 per cent and 40 per cent daygirls; those which have an almost evenly balanced number of boarders and daygirls; those which are mainly day schools but with between 5 per cent and 40 per cent boarders; and those which have daygirls only or only very few boarders. All but six of the schools which are wholly or mainly for daygirls have junior departments, most of which recruit from the age of 5; a majority of the other schools which take some daygirls have junior departments. The schools for boarders only which have junior departments recruit girls variously at 7, 8, 9 or 10 years of age to these departments, but none accept girls younger than 7; there are only very few girls younger than 9 who are boarders in any of these schools. Table III shows the number of schools in each category and the numbers with and without junior departments.

TABLE III

Boarding character of girls' public schools and whether with or without junior departments

Number of schools

Boarding Only		Mainly Boarding		Boarding and Day		Mainly Day		Day Only		All GBGSA Independent	
with	with-out	with	with-out	with	with-out	with	with-out	with	with-out	with	with-out
12	31	20	15	15	3	26	1	24	5*	97	55*
43		35		18		27		29		152	

Source: GBGSA files and *List of Independent Schools in England and Wales recognized as efficient, List* 70 (1965). London: H.M. Stationery Office, 1966.

* One of these schools has a separate but closely associated preparatory school.

Some of the schools are very old foundations; Christ's Hospital Girls' School goes back to 1552 and ten of the 152 schools were founded before 1800. Table IV shows the date of foundation according to type of school.

TABLE IV

Dates of foundation of girls' public schoools

Number of schools

Date of Foundation	Boarding Only and Mainly Boarding	Boarding and Day	Day Only and Mainly Day	Total
1500–1599	1	—	—	1
1600–1699	1	—	—	1
1700–1799	5	1	2	8
1800–1849	8	1	4	13
1850–1859	33	6	33	72
1900 or later	30	10	17	57
Total	78	18	56	152

Source: GBGSA files.

The Girls' Public Schools Today

By comparison with schools in the maintained system the girls' public schools are mostly small. Only seven schools have more than 600 pupils even when junior and senior departments are taken together. In general, the larger schools are among those founded between 1850 and 1899 during the great pioneering period of girls' secondary education. Sites were not as restricted and difficult to obtain then as they became later and capital costs were relatively low. Only one girls' public school established since 1920 has more than 400 pupils and most have fewer than 300. The number of girls in 1967 in the 152 girls' public schools including their junior departments is set against the schools' dates of foundation in Table V.

TABLE V

Date of foundation against size (senior with junior departments)

Number of schools

Girls in School	1500	1600	1700	1800	1850	1900	1920	1940	Totals
Number of Schools	1	1	8	15	69	28	23	7	152
800					2				2
700					1				1
600			1		2	1			4
500					5				5
400			1		18	4		1	24
300			3	6	17	1	5		32
200			3	7	13	13	12	2	50
100	1			2	11	8	6	3	31
		1				1		1	3

Date of Foundation

124

The Girls' Public Schools Today

Table VI shows the religious denomination of the schools. Most of the schools accept girls who are not of the religious persuasion of the school. The schools which are listed as undenominational or interdenominational have no specific religious foundation, but all hold religious services based on Christian ethics. None of the girls' public schools as far as is known, and certainly none of the schools for which full details are available on the files of the GBGSA, excuse girls from religious observance on the grounds of agnosticism or atheism, but possibly no parents have ever asked for their daughters to be excused for these reasons. Only eight Roman Catholic independent schools are at present members of the GBGSA, largely because Roman Catholic schools have always had their own associations and until recently have not applied for membership. The Roman Catholic convent schools will be discussed separately in the next chapter—

TABLE VI

Religious denomination of girls' public schools

Number of schools

	Boarding Only	Mainly Boarding	Boarding and Day	Mainly Day	Day Only	All Schools
Undenominational and Interdenominational	6	6	3	12	9	36
Church of England	30	24	12	11	20	97
Roman Catholic	4	1	1	2	—	8
Methodist	2	3	—	1	—	6
Other denominations	1	1	2	1	—	5
All schools	43	35	18	27	29	152

Source: GBGSA files.

The Girls' Public Schools Today

taken together they have nearly the same number of pupils as the girls' public schools.

More than half of the girls' public schools are in the Metropolitan area or the south of England defined as explained in the footnote to Table VII, which shows the distribution of the schools in broadly defined regions.

TABLE VII

Regional distribution of girls' public schools

Number of schools

	Boarding Only	Mainly Boarding	Boarding and Day	Mainly Day	Day Only	Total
Scotland	—	2	—	5	1	8
North*	5	2	1	4	7	19
Midlands*	17	8	1	6	4	36
Metropolitan*	—	1	—	5	9	15
South*	21	22	16	7	8	74
Total	43	35	18	27	29	152

Source: GBGSA files.

* The regions are defined as combinations of the regions used by the Department of Education and Science, of which full details are given in *Statistics of Education Part I*, 1965. The following combinations are used:
   North: Northern, Yorkshire (East and West Ridings) and North Western.
   Midlands: North Midland, Midland, Eastern and Wales.
   Metropolitan: Metropolitan.
   South: South Eastern, Southern and South Western.

The map on page 12 gives a more precise distribution and shows how the schools are clustered around London and in the Home Counties, with other groups in or near Malvern and Bristol and three day schools in the north on Tyneside. There are huge areas of the country, including all Wales other than North Wales, where there are no girls' independent public day or boarding schools. Many of the smaller girls' public boarding schools are in stately homes converted for use as a school and standing in spacious grounds. Almost all the boarding schools, large or small, have either as boarding houses or for school use buildings which were not designed originally for school purposes. Some of these buildings are exceptionally attractive and have great architectural merit, but few of them are as easy or economical to manage as new purpose-built premises would be.

THE GIRLS

The next tables show the number of girls in the schools grouped in various ways. Toward the end of 1966 the Public Schools Commission sent a general questionnaire to all the public schools, and copies of the completed questionnaire are being returned to the GBGSA. Copies of the schools' registers of pupils giving the number of girls on roll in each age group in January 1967 are being sent by request to the GBGSA for record purposes. By the end of April 1967, completed copies of the Public School Commission's questionnaire had been received from 126 of the 152 schools and the school registers (one of which was incomplete) from 150 schools. Questionnaires *and* registers were received from 124 schools. Information in the tables which follow and the descriptions of the schools' work and the headmistresses' comments have been collated from the questionnaires and registers (which relate to 1967) for the schools from which these were received, supplemented where necessary from statistics given in the *List of Independent Schools in England and Wales recognised as efficient, List 70* (1965). Numbers in the schools and in the various age groups fluctuate considerably from year to year and even from term to term, particularly in the boarding schools where the number of recruits at any one time is normally (though not necessarily precisely) determined by the number of leavers. As the general picture only is being aimed at here and any distortion caused by supplementing the numbers of pupils on roll in 1967 in 150 schools by the numbers on roll in 1965 for the remaining two schools is unlikely to be significant.

An estimate of the number of boarders and daygirls aged under 11 and 11-and-over in GBGSA schools (using a combination of 1967 returns and the 1965 *List 70*) is given in Table VIII.

There are about six times as many daygirls as boarders in the junior departments of the 150 girls' public schools for which 1967 figures were available, but about 30 per cent more boarders than daygirls in the senior departments. The greater number of girls under 11 years of age in the day schools and schools which are mainly day schools shows clearly.

Table I (page 32) showed that there were 229,539 girls of all ages in independent schools in the United Kingdom in 1965. The total of 47,930 girls shown in Table VIII thus indicates that just over one in five of the girls in all independent schools are in the girls' public schools.

The up-to-date information for 1967 for the 150 schools has been used in conjunction with estimates of the size of junior and senior departments from totals given in *List 70* (1965) for the remaining two schools to arrive at an estimate of the size of the senior departments in 1967 of all the 152 girls' public schools. The size of the senior departments in the schools divided according to boarding type is given in Table IX.

One third of the schools have fewer than 200 girls in senior departments and another third have between 200 and

TABLE VIII

Estimate of the number of boarders and day-girls aged under 11 and 11-and-over in GBGSA schools (the girls' public schools) in 1967

Number of girls

	Type of School		Boarding Only and Mainly Boarding	Boarding and Day	Day Only and Mainly Day	Total
The 150 schools for which details for 1967 were available	Number of schools		77	18	55	150
	Under eleven	Boarders	933	158	215	1,306
		Day-girls	689	849	6,577	8,115
		Total	1,622	1,007	6,792	9,421
	Eleven and over	Boarders	17,446	2,321	1,737	21,504
		Day-girls	1,691	2,074	12,859	16,624
		Total	19,137	4,395	14,596	38,128
	Total boarders		18,379	2,479	1,952	22,707
	Total day-girls		2,337	2,923	19,436	24,696
	Total		20,716	5,402	21,388	47,403
The two other GBGSA schools from *List 70* (1965)	Number of schools		1	—	1	2
	Boarders		134	—	—	134
	Day-girls		40	—	250	290
	Total		174	—	250	424
All GBGSA schools estimate	Number of schools		78	18	56	152
	Boarders		18,513	2,479	1,952	22,944
	Day-girls		2,377	2,923	19,686	24,986
	Total		20,890	5,402	21,638	47,930

Source: GBGSA files (1967) supplemented by *List 70* (1965), H.M. Stationery Office, 1966.

TABLE IX

Size of senior departments of the girls' public schools

Number of schools

Number of girls aged eleven-and-over	Boarding	Mainly Boarding	Boarding and Day	Mainly Day	Day	Total
Up to 200	13	15	8	4	14	54
200 to 299	19	14	4	16	4	57
300 to 399	7	2	5	4	7	25
400 to 499	4	3	—	3	3	13
500 to 599	—	—	1	—	—	1
600 to 699	—	—	—	—	1	1
700 to 799	—	—	—	—	—	—
800 and over	—	1	—	—	—	1
Total Schools	43	35	18	27	29	152

Source: *List 70* (1965). H.M. Stationery Office, 1966, and GBGSA files.

300 girls. Only three schools have more than 500 girls aged 11-and-over, and only one of these, Cheltenham Ladies' College with 822 girls, has more than 800. All discussions so far about maintained schools has indicated that no secondary school of less than at least 800 pupils can offer a full range of academic and non-academic courses for pupils of all abilities. The small size of the majority of girls' public schools (and, as will be seen, of most other girls' independent schools) seems therefore to rule out any possibility of any of them becoming comprehensive schools in the modern meaning of the term unless amalgamations or linked schools are, in what must surely be most exceptional instances, possible.

Full details of the school rolls for January 1967 were available for 149 schools; the number of girls of each age range of 11-and-over in these schools, divided according to the size of their senior departments, is shown in Table X.

The 38,000 girls aged 11-and-over in these 149 schools

The Girls' Public Schools Today

is 79·2 per cent of the estimated total number given in Table VIII of 47,930 girls in all the 152 girls' public schools. This indicates that the number of 13-year-old girls in the girls' public schools is about 7,850, that is, about 40 per cent of the 19,948 girls shown in Table I to be attending independent schools in the United Kingdom in 1965. This suggests that just over 2 per cent of girls aged 13 are attending girls' independent public schools, compared with about 2·7 per cent of boys aged 13 attending boys' independent public schools.

There is a wide variation in the number of girls staying on at school beyond 16 between different schools within each of the five categories of school: day only, mainly day, boarding

TABLE X

Number of girls aged 11-and-over by age in 149 GBGSA schools by size

Number of girls

Pupils	400 and over	300 to 399	200 to 299	100 to 199	Total
No. of Schools	16	25	57	51	149
Age of Pupils:					
11	820	1,073	1,722	960	4,575
12	1,061	1,307	2,198	1,203	5,769
13	1,288	1,366	2,257	1,332	6,243
14	1,297	1,368	2,327	1,391	6,383
15	1,263	1,346	2,215	1,287	6,111
16	1,138	1,194	1,780	998	5,110
17	848	775	981	497	3,101
18 and over	163	151	252	108	674
11 and over	7,888	8,585	13,721	7,711	37,966

Source: GBGSA files.

and day, boarding and boarding only. As is to be expected, the larger the school the greater in general is the percentage of girls staying on until 17 or 18, although there are notable exceptions. For example, Queen's College, London, although a school of only 254 pupils including three girls aged 10, has more girls of 18 and over than aged 13 and more than half the pupils are aged 16 and over. Moreover many of those of the smaller schools which have few girls older than 16 are doing a thoroughly good job. Pupils from the boarding schools may leave to go to the sixth forms of maintained or independent day schools, usually on the advice of the headmistress when sixth-form courses in

TABLE XI

Estimate of percentage of the 13-year-olds staying on until 16, 17 and 18 years of age in girls' public schools and other schools

	No. of Schools	16's as percentage of 13's	17's as percentage of 13's	18 and over as percentage of 13's	Totals Aged 13
Over 399	16	88·2	65·8	12·6	1,288
300–399	25	87·4	56·7	11·0	1,366
200–299	57	78·8	43·5	11·2	2,257
100–199	51	74·9	37·3	8·1	1,332
GBGSA	149	81·9	49·7	10·8	6,243
All recognized independent schools		73·8	38·1	8·9	15,209
Other		54·5	20·0	9·1	4,171
Direct grant grammar		79·9	63·3	17·4	7,892
Maintained grammar		73·6	51·7	15·7	57,642
All maintained schools		24·6	13·0	3·6	292,281
All schools		28·6	15·4	4·3	319,553

Source: *Statistics of Education, Part I, 1965*, London: H.M. Stationery Office, 1966, and GBGSA files.

TABLE XII

Number of girls of 16-and-over in girls' public schools

Number of schools

Number of girls of 16-and-over	Boarding	Mainly Boarding	Boarding and Day	Mainly Day	Day	Total
Over 99	5	4	2	5	5	21
75–99	6	—	3	2	4	15
50–74	11	12	4	6	4	37
25–49	15	16	7	14	11	63
fewer than 25	6	1	2	—	4	13
Total schools	43	33	18	27	28	149

Source: GBGSA files.

particular subjects cannot be provided, at least at the standards required to secure entrance to a university of first choice. Girls who have been at boarding school for four or five years often benefit by becoming day pupils for a final one or two years of sixth-form work. Similarly, girls at direct grant and independent day schools may profit by a final two years in a boarding school. This interchange is becoming increasingly common but is not evident in the bare statistical returns from an individual school.

Girls of 14 form the largest age group in schools of all sizes but, as the 13-year age group has customarily been used as the base for calculating the percentage of pupils staying on at school beyond the compulsory school leaving age, the number of girls aged 13 is used as a base here also. Table XI expresses the number of girls in the 149 schools aged 16, 17 and 18 who are still in school as percentages of the number of girls aged 13 in school taken from Table X. More strictly, the number of girls aged 16 in school should be expressed as a percentage of the number of girls aged 13 in school three years earlier, but these figures are not available and the present method, used consistently, gives a good guide for comparison with girls in maintained schools.

Most of the schools recruit fewer than thirty girls each year (that is, in educational parlance, less than one-form entry) and they therefore have no streaming in the ordinary sense of the word, and there is no strict definition in some schools of the sixth form. Many of the girls take ordinary level of the GCE as under-age candidates before the age of 16. To give the most generous interpretation of the size of sixth forms we can count all girls aged 16, 17 or 18-and-over as sixth-formers and thus gain some idea of the size of sixths. Table XII shows the 149 schools used in Tables X and XI divided according to the number of girls in each school aged 16 or over.

THE BOARDING SCHOOLS

The boarding schools have great flexibility in the age of entry, many of them accepting girls when there are suitable vacancies at any age after 11. Some schools have a deliberate policy of recruiting at 16 direct to sixth forms, and the numbers coming in midway through secondary education are increasing. Late entry is however more typical of the smaller schools and particularly those which have a big intake from overseas. The parents of these girls are mostly British, serving in the armed forces or the diplomatic corps, or executives of industrial or commercial firms sent abroad for two or three years—a facet of British business life which is becoming increasingly common. The schools also accept daughters of non-British parents whose native language may not be English. There are also an increasing number of American girls coming to spend one or two years in British boarding schools, some because their parents are over here and some because the experience is deemed valuable in itself. As many as half the annual intake of a few of the smaller schools come from overseas, and several schools regularly have an intake of up to a third of their pupils with parents abroad: the average for a random sample of thirty-two boarding schools is just less than one third. Slightly fewer than half of the girls at the boarding schools whose homes are in the British Isles live within fifty miles of the school.

Some of the schools have long waiting lists, but in the main parents seem to put their daughters' names down only three or four years before the date desired for entry. No real assessment of waiting lists is possible, but headmistresses say that when fees have to be substantially raised there is nowadays a sharp withdrawal of names. This is probably more true of the girls' than of the boys' schools.

Arrangements about entrance examinations and qualifications are very flexible. Although there is a common entrance examination which several schools use, a great many exceptions are made, and the headmistresses have absolute freedom to accept girls entirely on their own judgement. A daughter of an old girl is almost always accepted if there is a vacancy and if there is no reason to believe that she could not benefit by the type of education offered.

Few of the boarding schools have arrangements with local education authorities for a regular entry of girls from the maintained system; at one school where an arrangement does exist none had in fact been sent by the authority for several years. Several of the schools do regularly recruit, on a full fee-paying basis, girls who come direct from maintained schools either at 11 or later. One small school in Sussex with only 150 pupils which has boarders and daygirls had pupils from six different counties supported by local education authority grants; they were entered by the parents and not by the county authorities, the grants having been negotiated by the parents with the authorities after the girls had been entered or had already entered the school.

The average number of hours a week spent in study under the direction of a teacher, in private study, in organized games, athletics and physical education and in homework varies widely between schools. The time spent under the direction of a teacher by those preparing for GCE O-level, for example, varies from 18 or 19 hours to 26 hours. In general, the smaller the school the fewer the hours spent in study under the direction of a teacher, whether at ordinary or advanced level or in the younger age groups. The boarding schools have very flexible school hours, and timetables are almost all 'individual', at least after the age of 14.

Music is an important feature of almost all the girls' public schools and at the boarding schools it is usual for girls to have music lessons during the normal hours of the school day in carefully arranged free periods. The boarding schools thus often have a proportionately very large full-time or part-time music staff who teach at any or all times of the day, the lessons being charged as an extra over and above the school fees. There is no equivalent to this in the maintained day schools, where individual music lessons in school hours are rare, although some schools are experimenting with allowing third—and fourth—year pupils to have music lessons once a week, missing a different class each week in rotation, and many maintained schools organize group instrumental teaching as a normal part of the timetable.

The staffing ratio of the girls' public boarding schools is hard to assess accurately. They make great use of part-time staff and untrained graduate married women living within driving distance of the school and coming to teach at hours to suit their domestic commitments. Resident staff with tutorial and out-of-school duties also may teach only part-time, adjusting their day's work to suit girls' timetables. Most girls who are preparing for ordinary level in the GCE are taught in sets of about twenty for the popular subjects—English, French, biology; in slightly smaller groups for mathematics, geography and other less common subjects, and in very small groups for unusual subjects, Russian, Spanish and, nowadays, Latin. The sets for advanced-level study will be correspondingly smaller except in the largest schools where almost all attempt advanced-level GCE. Comparison with a large maintained grammar school of over 600 girls shows a striking similarity in the average size of ordinary-level and advanced-level teaching sets for the various GCE subjects. The number of different combinations of subjects offered at advanced level also varies, naturally, with the size of the school, but in general it is plain that in the public boarding schools a girl can take any combination of subjects that she chooses provided that there is staff in the school with relevant qualifications. And even when staff is not available for some particular subject, arrangements will usually be made for private tuition outside the school. The flexibility is probably more evident in the relatively small schools than in the much larger schools where a lot of exceptions may upset the normal routine.

Most schools offer a wide range of sixth-form courses not leading to the advanced-level GCE examination, and again it seems that the smaller schools are the more imaginative, possibly because flexibility is easier and they are not as closely orientated toward university entrance as the larger schools. Courses mentioned include music appreciation, art appreciation, man and his inheritance, American history, structure of society, history of the cinema, modern drama, dressmaking, cookery, architecture, Christian belief, contemporary literature, modern politics, classical background, the Communist World, St John and Red Cross, English of everyday life, personal relationships, economics, nursing and hygiene, human biology and, of course, for a few girls, typing and shorthand.

Many schools, probably the majority, are experimenting with the new mathematics syllabuses, Nuffield science and the new methods of teaching modern languages. The girls' schools have readily taken to the new Certificate of Secondary Education for those who are not able to take ordinary-level GCE in their stride. As this is only the second year of the CSE not many of the schools mentioned it in answering the questionnaire.

Some schools offer as many as five foreign languages including Latin; although Latin is often a strong subject in the Roman Catholic schools, it has never held pride of place in girls' schools. Mathematics appears to be no weaker in the public schools than in girls' schools generally, but when a girl does offer advanced level mathematics she is likely to have virtually individual teaching or to be in a very small teaching set and as a consequence may do exceptionally well.

Broadcast television and radio are often included as part of normal teaching, but in none of the replies to the questionnaires were teaching machines mentioned. The independent schools have not the money to spare to go in for educational technology in a big way until its value is proved beyond doubt.

There have been a great many changes and experiments in curricula over the past five years, all of which reflect a general widening of school work and interests.

The Girls' Public Schools Today

Time spent in religious worship varies greatly: those schools which have a charter or other instrument of foundation which prescribes a particular denomination tend to spend more time. Some give a bare ten minutes each weekday to a usually undenominational religious assembly service with an hour spent in religious observance on Sundays; others of specific denominations spend up to twenty-one hours a week in religious observance with two church services on Sundays. Special arrangements are made for girls whose faith is different from that of the school.

There is a very wide range of extra-curricular activities. Most of the boarding schools, except those which are geographically isolated, take part in local activities. Guides, Brownies, Red Cross work, youth clubs and Sunday school teaching, music, drama and art clubs, public speaking competitions, welfare work in hospitals and with handicapped children or old people are all mentioned repeatedly. The schools combine with local schools in forming orchestras, for plays, tennis, team-game matches, United Nations, Christian Student Movement, and all manner of societies and other clubs. There seem to be no limits to the willingness to forge links with local schools and to take part in local community activities other than those set by lack of opportunity or time. In some areas there is a great deal of mutual help with amenities and with staff for specialist subjects between neighbouring public schools, in the few instances where they are not too far distant, and also with local secondary schools.

Most schools take several daily and Sunday newspapers and a large selection of journals. *The Times*, *Guardian* and *Telegraph*, *Sunday Times* and *Observer* are mentioned by nearly all schools. In some schools the libraries are poor, but in others they are good (judged by the number of books) or even magnificent; there is one library with well over 30,000 non-fiction books as well as a large stock of fiction.

Boarding houses vary in size and in organization. Where they were purpose-built toward the end of the last century they tend to be for units of forty to sixty girls with dormitories for up to ten. Most now have a number of single rooms or 'study-bedroom cubicles' for senior girls, and some of the schools favoured single and double rooms or small dormitories as a matter of policy from the start; several are converting dormitories into divided single rooms so that senior girls can have more privacy than used to be possible.

Rules about visiting and about going home during the term are being greatly relaxed. Sixth-formers in most schools now are allowed to go out with parents or other visitors almost without restriction so long as work is done and the demands are reasonable. Plainly schools vary greatly in the extent to which they allow this kind of freedom but the questionnaires show that there have been big changes within the past few years. Only a few schools mention weekly boarding, but perhaps more evidence on this may emerge at a later stage.

The number of resident domestic staff in the boarding schools seems to be very small. Pupils have to do a good many chores themselves, which may or may not be good training. Girls have never, even in the past, been spoilt in this respect, but severe shortage of domestic staff has considerably altered the way in which meals can be served and makes the public boarding schools today very different institutions from fifty or even twenty years ago. As everybody has to lend a hand— teaching staff, sixth-formers and new girls alike—there is less formality in relationships at every level; fagging was not mentioned in the questionnaire by any school.

A surprising amount of new building and alteration to

buildings is going on all the time. Despite lack of capital a majority of the schools seem to have managed to undertake some modernization of either teaching or residential accommodation. Converting dormitories into single study-bedrooms has already been mentioned. Some schools have improved their laboratories since the closing of the Industrial Fund which gave financial help for this; some have built swimming pools or gymnasia using money subscribed by parents, old girls and friends; several headmistresses mention that it has been found possible to dispense with outdated sanatoria and to convert these for alternative use, often as sixth-form or 'student' centres.

All the headmistresses have something to say about changes in the curriculum—the proposed introduction of the CSE, for example, of new mathematics and the School Mathematics Project, of Nuffield Science projects, of 'direct teaching' and use of tape-recorders in modern languages, expansion of general studies, orchestral work (one school has started a guitar orchestra), educational cruises, bellringing, choral work with local societies, careers conventions in collaboration with neighbouring schools, more field work in geography and so on. There is frequent mention of broadcast television used as an educational medium.

There is less emphasis on team games and usually games are no longer compulsory for senior girls. Cricket, where it is still played, appears to be finally on the way out, although one school for which it was stated that cricket had 'been dropped' added a reservation that there was still a cricket club. Golf, fencing, judo, winter swimming, winter tennis, ballet, modern dance, squash, table tennis, roller skating, ice skating, riding (one school has ponies of its own) and driving lessons; rock climbing, life-saving, first-aid classes, athletics, trampoline, canoeing, sailing, even skiing (in Scotland)—all

these activities appear in the lists of major changes introduced during the past five years.

Routines affecting the pattern of the girls' daily life have
been greatly relaxed in nearly all schools. One school now
allows senior girls to prepare their own breakfast and tea
and to work in their study-bedrooms during free time; they
can wear their own clothes and turn out their own lights and
have the use of a student centre exclusively to themselves
with freedom to entertain and to go out with friends.

Another headmistress writes that the whole nature of the
top of the school has changed in recent years, with more
flexibility, more choice for the girls about what they do
and more reliance on self-discipline. Almost all schools
mention a relaxation about school uniform, at least for senior
girls, and one head writes that hats are no longer compulsory
except on formal occasions. It would be a sad day if there
were to be no school hats at all—what then would girls
have to throw to the winds on the day they leave? Some
schools are more generous than others about time allowed for
watching television, but the restriction is not a matter of
principle, merely that there is work to be done and there is
not unlimited time.

The questionnaire did not ask for examination results, but
it did ask for detailed information of the examination successes, other qualifications and destinations of all leavers in
the summer of 1966. The Commission itself will presumably
in due course give a detailed statistical analysis of these
returns. A great many girls go to universities from the public
schools —particularly from the larger schools which have a
tradition of preparing for university entrance. Surprisingly
few leavers from the boarding schools go to the colleges of
education to train for teaching, but their normal route into
teaching is through the universities. Girls who do not do well

enough to get into university from school at their first try at perhaps 17 or just 18, and who want to leave, tend to go to the private coaching establishments or to a local authority college to improve their advanced-level GCE passes. Many girls from the boarding schools go into hospital training of one kind or another and many go to universities abroad, to the Sorbonne or to Geneva or, increasingly often now if they can somehow raise the money, to an American university or college. Girls from the smaller schools may leave at 16 to go to local authority day schools to complete sixth-form courses. This is usually on the advice of their own headmistress if a desired course cannot be provided. Also, as has been said earlier, girls often do not want to stay longer than four, or at most five, years in the same boarding school, and to come home to school at 16 may be as good a move as going away at 16 for two years at a boarding school can be for those who have had all previous education at a day school. A few go into articled apprenticeships to study for law or accountancy without first seeking degrees. The schools seem to be well aware of the facilities available for school-leavers in the colleges of further education, particularly in art and in sub-jects related to art, but a great many girls go from the public schools to the private secretarial colleges, the names of a few of which appear repeatedly in the lists of destinations of school leavers.

The headmistresses were asked to say to what extent, and in what ways, they would consider that the head and teaching staff in a public school have greater freedom than the staff of a maintained school. First and foremost head-mistresses value the freedom to appoint (and dismiss) assistant staff and to run their own school without reference to governors and without having to comply to some 'committee policy' which might appear arbitrary or inapplicable to their special needs. They value having complete freedom to spend available funds as they think best and to have an active part in the planning and supervision of new buildings, but they readily admit that to be seriously short of money is at least as restrictive as to have governors or committees exercising active control. Heads of public schools have more responsibility about financial matters and therefore, inevitably, more worries too—some of them know enough of the maintained system to appreciate that there is some advantage in having finance cared for elsewhere and therefore to have more time and energy left for concentration on education itself.

The heads seem to feel strongly about textbooks, pointing out that they are able to change these as often as required— this because girls in public schools have to pay for their own textbooks and class materials, whereas in maintained schools these are provided by the local education authorities through a capitation allowance which is spent at the discretion of the head. Some local authorities are more liberal about textbooks than others, and freedom about choice of textbooks in independent schools of course depends on the parents' ability to pay for them.

Freedom to arrange school holidays and the length of the school day is also much appreciated. There is a statutory minimum number of days in the year which constitute compulsory schooling, but independent schools can arrange these days when they wish, and this is a great convenience, especially as regards half-term holidays and whether or not to allow a term to overrun Easter or Whitsun.

Some headmistresses commented that the relationship with parents is closer in independent than in maintained schools. Certainly parents will have made a deliberate choice and will have spent time in visiting the school and getting to know the headmistress before their daughters first come. The heads thus have a real knowledge of all parents which is rare in maintained schools. In all normal circumstances parents will visit their daughters and the school at least every year and usually every term. The heads must be responsive to the views of parents if support is to be held; if a girl does not make satisfactory progress parents can and will take her away and send her somewhere else. But there is little if any interference or pressure of any kind; approval or disapproval is expressed by sending or not sending a daughter to the school. The governors may try to influence a head to make changes in this direction or that, but usually the initiative comes from the headmistress herself. Governors of independent schools feel themselves to be custodians of freedom and are rarely influenced by political or other extraneous considerations in governing a school.

Several headmistresses said that freedom from the excessive form-filling of the maintained system was valuable— which was remarkable coming on the sixteenth page of a huge and detailed questionnaire!

The girls' schools rely greatly on part-time staff. The headmistresses of the public schools not only make all the appointments, but they are able to negotiate salary scales for part-time staff, and, with complete freedom to act without consultation, they can engage teachers on the spot at any time of the year and without formalities and delay. In this way they can collect about them teaching staff who might otherwise not be teaching or might slip through the local authority net because of the complications of quota arrangements and so on in the maintained schools. Few girls' schools pay over Burnham scales, rigorously interpreted. School work and timetable can be adapted to suit the needs of the staff; they can be given leave of absence according to judgement and are not expected to remain on the premises throughout the school day, which is obligatory in the maintained system. One public boarding school some two hours' train journey from London allows resident staff to spend two days with the intervening night out of the school altogether once a fortnight—an immense attraction to young and older members of staff who repay the school with extra energy and enthusiasm.

The heads also regard their freedom to decide which girls shall be admitted to the schools as important—and also their freedom to ask for a girl's withdrawal from the school. This sanction is scarcely ever used. If a girl is unwilling to submit to the normal discipline of a school, she will not hesitate to try to get herself removed and can usually find another school—there has to be a different philosophy in a maintained school which is obliged to accept all comers and cannot dismiss a girl. This could be a big bone of contention if some agreement is arrived at whereby more girls are sent by local education authorities to the public schools. Normally there will be agreement between the sending authority and the headmistress of the receiving school, and headmistresses are notably generous in their willingness to help all girls, in particular those who have difficult home backgrounds. But the headmistress of an independent school is very much head of a family and there must be harmony; unless she has the ultimate right to accept or refuse a girl no scheme could operate successfully.

The final question was whether headmistresses thought that there were any significant differences between boys' and girls' schools not previously brought out. Many headmistresses left this question unanswered presumably on the grounds that they had little or no personal experience of boys' schools. One head wrote rather laconically that the questionnaire did not seem to bring out any differences—as indeed in the wording of the questions, if not in the answers, it did not. Several headmistresses mentioned that discipline concerning out-of-school activities has to be more strict in a girls' than in a boys' school, but they added that, inside the confines of the school, discipline for girls can be much less strict. One headmistress commented that, whereas boys have to be goaded into work, girls more usually have to be curbed from excessive zeal. The most frequent comment was the slightly wistful observation that whereas headmasters of boys' public schools had separate houses and (usually) wives to help, headmistresses very rarely have a separate house and their life is thereby harder and much more closely wrapped up in the school. The lack of married quarters for housemistresses also restricts recruitment and big changes of policy are having to be made to overcome this difficulty, including the appointment of non-teaching housemistresses.

THE DAY SCHOOLS

The day schools show much the same pattern of advance as the boarding schools, but there is less scope for dramatic change in organization or in discipline. There are the big public day schools which are comparable to direct grant schools; most of these have some pupils whose fees are paid by local authorities. The difference financially between being independent and having direct grant status is that there is no capitation allowance or subsidy direct from the Department of Education and Science and there is no grant from the Department to make up fees on a sliding scale related to income for parents in low income groups. The public day schools settle their own fees without having to ask permission, and they can expand, if they can find the money, as they wish—which direct grant and aided schools may not.

The smaller public day schools play an important role in filling gaps in the nation's education system. Some of them are schools of special character which were founded to meet particular needs—schools with ancient foundations which do not fit into the maintained system but yet have values of their own—church schools, for example, which offer the same type of education for girls as choir schools offer for boys. Many of these schools have an arrangement with the local authorities for accepting sponsored pupils.

An analysis of the questionnaires returned by head-mistresses of the day schools follows the same lines as for the boarding schools. Class sizes appear to be comparable, school-leavers' destinations are much the same from schools of similar size although more girls from day than from boarding schools go to local authority colleges of further education rather than private secretarial colleges. Where sixth forms are small, many school leavers will go at 16 to other larger schools to benefit by a greater choice of subjects at pre-university level. In general, the headmistresses of the day schools have fewer comments to make about recent changes, probably because there is less time at their disposal and, during school hours, there has to be more concentration on class teaching.

Headmistresses greatly value the freedom of being independent—in appointing staff, in arranging the school day, in choosing textbooks and so on. Many heads arrange timetables so that every member of staff can have a free half-day each week. In a good local authority the freedom given to headmistresses to run their own schools can be considerable, but there may be unexpected and sometimes niggling regulations which cannot be ignored. There is also always the threat that a change of committee control may directly affect the policy of a local authority school; head teachers and other members of teaching staffs are then expected to be 'loyal to the service' rather than to the school in which all their emotional involvement and interest may be centred. This possibility of being overruled in matters of principle and of schools being treated as though they were commercial enterprises, rather than institutions with a soul and built through the spirit, weakens the maintained system today and threatens to rob flourishing schools of their life force. The independent day schools are part of the remaining reserve line for parents who do not find what they want in the maintained system and, apart from the intrinsic worth of what they achieve, they form an essential bastion of a free democracy.

CHAPTER SIX

Other Independent Girls' Schools

THE INDEPENDENT CONVENT SCHOOLS

No picture of girls' independent schools in this country can be complete without special mention of the independent Roman Catholic convent schools. There are about 145 in England and Wales (Table XIII) and together they have some 43,000 pupils, nearly 7,000 of whom are boarders.

TABLE XIII

Boarding character of independent Roman Catholic convent schools

	Boarding Only	Mainly Boarding	Boarding and Day	Mainly Day	Day Only	Total
Schools	6	7	20	56	56	145
Boarders	880	1,040	1,930	2,966	72	6,888
Day-girls	8	262	2,230	15,130	18,529	36,159
All girls	888	1,302	4,160	18,096	18,601	43,047

Source: *The Directory of Catholic Schools and Colleges*, 29th edition, London: Paternoster Publications, 1966, and *List 70* (1965), H.M. Stationery Office.

All but 21 have junior departments taking pupils before the age of 11 and 80 take boarders (Table XIV).

Most of the convent schools other than those which have direct grant status are small, but some are not; one inde-

TABLE XIV

Boarding character of independent Roman Catholic convent schools with and without junior departments

Boarding Only		Mainly Boarding		Boarding and Day		Mainly Day		Day Only		Total	
with	with-out	with	with-out	with	with-out	with	with-out	with	with-out	with	with-out
2	4	6	1	19	1	52	4	45	11	124	21
6		7		20		56		56		145	

Source: *The Directory of Catholic Schools and Colleges*, 29th edition, London: Paternoster Publications, 1966, and *List 70* (1965), H.M. Stationery Office.

pendent convent day school has over 1,000 girls (Table XV).

The pupils in these schools are not necessarily all members of the Catholic faith; many non-Catholic parents go out of their way to seek a convent education for their daughters, believing that there is special merit in the kind of education and training offered. Fees in general are lower in the convent schools than in other independent schools, partly because many nuns have in the past taught without salaries, although the equivalent of the salaries that they would earn are now more usually credited to the Catholic Order or organization which is responsible for their school. Fees are usually varied to help Catholic children from families with low incomes; this means in effect that parents who can afford to pay high fees do so (knowingly and presumably willingly) for the benefit of those who cannot.

If the financial situation becomes too difficult for a convent school to continue, the only alternative open, other than closing the school and depriving Catholic children of a Catholic education, is to seek aided status. Some independent Catholic schools (and one Catholic public school in the past

TABLE XV

Size of independent Roman Catholic convent schools
(senior with junior departments)

Number of Schools

Girls in the Schools	Boarding Only	Mainly Boarding	Boarding and Day	Mainly Day	Day Only	Total Schools
1,000 and over					1	1
900					—	—
800					—	—
700					2	2
600				3	1	4
500				3	4	7
400			1	9	7	17
300	1	—	1	17	12	31
200	—	4	8	16	18	46
100	3	2	10	8	9	32
	2	1	—	—	2	5
Total	6	7	20	56	56	145

Source: *List 70* (1965), H.M. Stationery Office.

few months) are already having to do this. On the surface there may not seem great loss in coming under the local authority umbrella as an aided school but, immediately, the school becomes subject to all the regulations and controls of other maintained schools, with restrictions about settling policy and, at present, the whole question of being requested to reorganize in combination with other neighbouring schools into some form of comprehensive system—which may not at all meet the wishes of the governors or match the traditions and aims of a school's founders.

The scale of Roman Catholic provision in independent schools would create a formidable administrative and financial problem for any government that decided to insist on getting rid of the public schools. There are not far short of 100,000 girls in public schools and convent schools taken together, and the overlap between the two not mutually exclusive categories, in the type of education that they offer, in the size of schools and in standards of achievement, are so great that it would be totally unwarranted to take discriminatory action which affected one without regard to the other. Catholics who live in the West country and in other areas where they are in a small minority can only obtain a Catholic education for their daughters by sending them to a boarding school; and the Catholic schools which take boarders usually need to have daygirls also—and often non-Catholics as well—to make the school an educationally and economically viable unit.

These schools do not come under the direct terms of reference of the Public Schools Commission, but their contribution to the nation's education system cannot be ignored, nor does it seem possible that they can be integrated in any satisfactory way into local plans for comprehensive education, although some individual convent schools may be able to find methods of fitting in. All of them are and would be willing to accept girls from local authorities, but the local authorities do not show equal willingness to take up places where day school provision in aided schools is possible, and the Catholic authorities seem to prefer to see money spent on adding to and improving local aided schools with the 80 per cent subsidy for capital expenditure rather than having fees paid at independent convent schools.

There are also a great number of other independent secondary schools, including about forty co-educational secondary schools, many of them Quaker or other religious foundations, with over 10,000 boys and girls almost half of whom are boarders, which do an important job in educating the nation's children. The girls' public schools, the independent convent and other denominational schools probably account for well over two-thirds of the 20,000 or so 13-year-old girls shown in Table I to be attending independent recognized schools. To abolish them would be enormously expensive, apart from the gross interference with fundamental human rights that this would imply.

No description of the remaining recognized independent schools is possible here, for no detailed information is easily available; some no doubt are of poor quality and will have only just scraped into the list of those recognized as efficient, but parents do not have to send their daughters to inadequate independent schools, and schools which have little to offer will these days not last long; it can therefore be assumed that those that flourish have qualities which parents value even if educationists with their largely theoretical assessments sometimes judge them harshly.

PREPARATORY SCHOOLS AND DEPARTMENTS

A majority of girls attending public boarding schools have spent some time in independent preparatory schools or departments. In 1965 there were 100 girls' independent preparatory schools and 1,318 independent preparatory schools for girls and boys. Together, these schools were attended by 83,335 girls compared with 2,463,512 girls in maintained primary schools. In addition, 369 independent girls' secondary schools had junior departments and 376 other independent boys', girls' or co-educational 'secondary-and-primary' schools had junior departments which accepted boys and girls. In 1965 there were eighty-one direct grant girls' schools with junior departments or 'lower schools' in the United Kingdom and thirty-seven other direct grant lower schools taking boys and girls.* The total number of girls of primary school age in direct grant and independent schools or departments in the United Kingdom in 1965 (all unsubsidized from public funds) was 128,734, which was slightly fewer than the number of boys and almost exactly 5 per cent of girls in all primary schools or departments. As was shown in the previous chapter, 95 of the 152 girls' public schools have junior departments.

Except in the special circumstances when parents are abroad (and even then daughters more often than sons are left in the care of relatives) and where there is ill health at home, frequent moving of place of residence or other disturbances which make boarding almost essential, few parents think of sending their daughters to a boarding school before the secondary stage. The risk of girls becoming institutionalized through over-extended boarding education can be greater and, later on, more damaging to adult life than for boys. Moreover, girls seem to tire more quickly than boys of boarding school. The common experience of boarding schools with junior departments is that after about five years at one school away from home girls become restless and need a change of environment; if they have been boarders at the same school before 13 and certainly if before the age of

* Statistics of Education, Part One, 1965 (H.M.S.O.).

11, to persuade them to stay on into second-year or third-year sixth forms is correspondingly more difficult.

Parents may choose to send their daughters to one of the many independent day preparatory schools which provide education up to 11, 12 or 13. Most day preparatory schools have been obliged to aim at gaining for their pupils a 'pass in the local eleven-plus examination', a fee-paying place in a direct grant school or entrance to public school. This has been the main basis on which they have retained parents' confidence. Now that the eleven-plus examination is to disappear, the preparatory schools may lose some of their attraction, but this may also make entrance to direct grant grammar schools as fee-payers and to the leading public day and boarding schools even more competitive, if these schools are permitted still to recruit on ability, and then the coaching element of the day preparatory schools could become even more important than now in parents' eyes. Places in preparatory schools and departments which are attached to direct grant grammar schools and to independent schools are eagerly sought. The girls who gain these places have undeniable advantages when the time comes for transition to the senior schools. The future of these preparatory schools and departments is inextricably bound up with that of the direct grant and independent schools themselves.

The normal expectation of a girl in the junior department of a public day or boarding school or of a direct grant school is to proceed to the senior department or upper school. Only a few fail to do so in spite of competitive entry. For this reason when a girl has succeeded in gaining a place in one of these junior departments (perhaps at five years of age), the problem of making some other choice for secondary education does not often arise, unless boarding education is specifically sought. If a child has attended an 'unattached' private preparatory school the inference hitherto has been that unless a selective place is desired and gained in a maintained grammar school (a consideration which may soon no longer be relevant) or in a direct grant grammar school parents will expect to continue to pay for independent education at the secondary stage.

The preparatory schools may not have enjoyed their role of beating the eleven-plus, and freedom from this pressure by parents may help them. They may lose the children who came as it were for the wrong reasons—in order to be crammed or for snob value—but, if so, they may gain in freedom about how and what to teach, and the best of them may thus develop new strengths and new attractions. Their principal educational advantage over the maintained primary schools is their very much smaller classes. Some have only a few full-time members of staff but put great reliance on part-time women graduates and on unqualified nongraduate assistants, who may be women of considerable cultural background. The headmistress of a good girls' preparatory school will almost always be a devoted teacher herself, otherwise she would never have become head of a private school in the first place. She will often have attracted and held one or two equally dedicated teachers. The full-time staff work long hours and give unstinted individual attention to the children in their care. They value the independent status of the school and the freedom this gives them to teach by methods in which they believe. The result at its best can be outstanding. All the children before they leave, even the dullest, will almost certainly have learnt how to work, how to read fluently and fast, how to spell, and how to write correct English in a good hand. They may also have been expected to have accumulated from their books a great deal of factual knowledge. This may be outmoded, but is not to be altogether scorned. A private preparatory school may or may not use the 'new' techniques of teaching primary mathematics, although many* have done so for years—before ever the state schools saw the light—but no child will leave without knowing multiplication tables. Maintained primary schools with all their modern methods and, in general, excellent facilities and equipment also achieve at their best spectacular results. The preparatory schools, much derided as they sometimes nowadays are, may equally teach by encouragement and through 'learning-by-doing', and equally they may make use of new ideas and new techniques when the head is convinced of their value. They may still insist on some learning by rote, but who is to say that this has not some value now as it used to have with earlier generations? Some so-called old-fashioned methods may still in the long run be worth preserving. Above all, the preparatory schools have to succeed with their children: if they do not, they quickly lose support and go out of business.

There is no association for girls' preparatory schools equivalent to the boys' schools' Incorporated Association of Preparatory Schools.

---

* I cannot refrain from remarking here that at my own kindergarten we learnt our mathematics with rods and pegs and home-made balances, and that I knew just why 2 × 3 was the same as 3 × 2 before I was six. We were taught 'sets' and one-to-one correspondence then. The whole school at that time was 'good at mathematics'.

CHAPTER SEVEN

Parental Attitudes and Choice of School

INFLUENCES

This is the era of the young. Thirty years ago girls at school looked forward to being grown-up and they dressed in imitation of their mothers. They resented short skirts as being childish and enjoyed no self-orientated teenage culture. They had little or no money of their own to spend and they were of only slight interest as a group to manufacturers and advertisers. Nowadays all this has changed. The girls and their boy friends set and lead the fashions. Mums try to keep up, wondering how short with decency they can reasonably allow their skirts to be—envying their daughters' warm gay stockings but usually unwilling to copy them except when away from public gaze.

The young, both boys and girls, are the trend setters—and most attractive and refreshing all this is. Design has never been more uninhibited or, often, more inspired. The independence and adventurous spirit of young people today is wholly stimulating. We may not like all that we see and hear of modern trends, but every period of history has had its black aspects and young people of each new generation in turn, creating their own *mores* and their own problems, find also their own partial solutions.

159

Parental Attitudes and Choice of School

What concerns us here is the effect of current trends among young people on the future of the public schools. If a boy is to go to a public school, parents have in the past planned for this almost from the day of the christening. Waiting lists for the best-known public schools, both boys' and girls', are still long; if parents want to be sure of their children gaining a place in due course at a leading public boarding school they must think about entering them very early. Some schools accept names at birth; others not before a child is 8 years old. Moreover, most parents have to begin to plan early if they are to initiate savings schemes to help to meet the expense later on. In America, where there are no automatic student grants for higher education, parents commonly take up insurance policies when their children are young to cover eventual costs of sending them to college. Here many parents who make up their minds from the beginning to send their children to public schools, other things being equal, nowadays use the same techniques. Government policies apart, the future of the public schools in the 1970's and 1980's therefore depends a great deal on the attitudes of young people who have only recently left school themselves and who are or soon will be the new generation of parents.

More than one half of all pupils at the public schools at present are believed to be children of parents who have not themselves attended public schools. None the less we do well to ask public school leavers for their views, making intelligent allowance for individual bias.

The girl at the public day school will probably not be either more or less critical of the education she receives than a girl at a direct grant day school. Many would welcome a curriculum which was less academically orientated, with more emphasis on a variety of forms of art, music, drama, social and domestic studies and current affairs as an integral part of the timetable rather than as subjects to be fitted in as lunchtime or after-school activities. The schemes of work for the first three years from 11 to 14 at a public day school may be liberal in design, but once the GCE looms ahead some of the schools concentrate almost exclusively on examination syllabuses. The girls' schools rarely risk allowing pupils to 'by-pass' ordinary level subjects and a timetable which aims at preparing a girl to take seven or more academic subjects at ordinary level leaves little time for other work and none at all for genuine leisure. Some schools insist on art, music or domestic science being offered as an ordinary-level subject in the GCE to ensure that the curriculum is never entirely dominated by traditional academic subjects. In the sixth forms, especially if General Studies is taken as an advanced-level subject, the curriculum of most girls' grammar schools becomes more liberal again—the girls' schools were and still are the leaders in developing 'general sixths' and programmes with a broad educational content for 'minority time'.* The girls' grammar schools have never specialized as early or as intensely as has been usual in some boys' grammar schools; it is, however, probably true to say that the independent girls' public day schools have concentrated more on examination successes than is characteristic of the public boarding schools, largely because at boarding school there is more time within which to arrange a balanced amalgam of academic and liberal activities.

Girls from some of the public boarding schools will say that there were too many petty rules and regulations, that they would have liked more possibility of privacy, more freedom to go to shops, more facilities to entertain, more opportunity to go to the theatre, cinema and to concerts. But these are

* See the Crowther Report.

old complaints and there is nowadays so much change in most schools that generalization is misleading. Some girls will say that there was not enough unallocated time to spend in leisure pursuits of their own choice. Again this is generalization and as true or false of girls' public boarding schools as of any other type of secondary school. Criticisms of this kind, although important, are not fundamental—where they are justified and where there is the will to make needed changes in the internal running of a school, heads and staff backed by understanding governing bodies can usually make them.

Girls from the public boarding schools readily appreciate the opportunity they have had to learn to live in a community whose values are stable and understood, to have been taught to fend for themselves with no 'running home to mother' and to have gained confidence by being given first small and gradually greater responsibilities within a secure and sympathetic environment. To educate for 'leadership' may nowadays be considered an aim with unfortunate social overtones—other schools, too, produce leaders. But the public boarding schools do this both deliberately and incidentally; the whole of school life is hierarchical—the senior pupils have authority which they are expected to use constructively, humanely and effectively in helping to run the houses and the school as a whole; and the younger pupils given small but real responsibilities from the beginning learn to serve and to respect authority in the certain knowledge that within what is for them foreseeable time they will themselves have to assume it. There is no problem in the public schools of early leaving; although a few pupils of course will leave before the sixths, the normal expectation is that every pupil will stay until at least 17 and thus all pupils will usually have their turn as senior members of house and school.

Parental Attitudes and Choice of School

The house system of most girls' public boarding schools is part of their ethos. Day schools copy this method of dividing a large school into manageable units, but day-school 'houses' are usually large, say 200 pupils or so, whereas the average size of house in the girls' boarding schools is forty. Every girl knows every other girl in the same house really well and a powerful spirit is engendered. A girls' boarding school of 400 divided into ten houses each with forty girls, all of whom normally remain in the same house for at least four and probably five years from 13 develops its own powerful educational influence that is indelible and affects attitudes and behaviour for the rest of a lifetime.

There is emphasis on self-discipline and on seeing a job through to the finish—both of which virtues can be inculcated more thoroughly at boarding school than in a day school. Self-reliance coupled with consideration for others is essential for reasonable survival and becomes habitual—nor is there the possibility of scrimshanking as there is for a girl at home who is allowed to be spoilt. Regular bedtime, balanced diets and time spent out of doors every day are routines which every adolescent girl should have, but few do have when they are at home. Overwork or too much 'swotting' for examinations is never allowed at a boarding school—house mistresses, who in nearly all girls' boarding schools are also members of the schools' academic teaching staffs, soon notice if a girl is having to work too hard to keep up with her lessons, and timetables are then immediately adjusted; because hours for preparation are controlled, at least for the younger girls, the necessity to work fast soon teaches concentration. A girl at a public school develops almost inevitably a sense of identity both with the school (as with any good school) and with the pioneering spirit of the origin of girls' secondary education. This does not mean a loss of femininity

—on the contrary, many girls' public schools pay special attention to the cultivation of feminine graces (and competence)—but a public school education does engender a habit of loyalty that comes when an identity is achieved with an institution or purpose beyond the narrow bounds of self. Loyalty to a country, a cause, a school, to one's family can all be great sources of strength and helpful props when wavering between right and wrong. Any good school inspires loyalty and so imposes its standards on its pupils: the public schools with their specific identities and histories are especially able to wield this lasting influence.

Girls are very sensitive to atmosphere; they show an odd mixture of independence and conformity and they need both if they are to grow to a full and satisfying maturity. They like to be 'different', to be noticed, to be liked, to be able to demonstrate independence—but they also want reassurance from time to time and to feel that they are in a well-ordered and even a protective society. They like to be 'in the swim' and they can be martyrs to fashion—about clothes and hairstyles or about the fundamental issues of going to college or university, of choice of career or occupation, of marrying early or the desired size of family. The public boarding schools can provide exactly the right environment for some girls, giving them freedom to develop their individuality, to find their own strength and weaknesses within a secure community, giving them the confidence that they need in adult life to play their full role in the home and at work as independent thinkers and leaders. A girl who has recently left school and who is savouring the new freedoms of fully adult life may pass through a phase of scepticism, but the school if it has done its job well will have made an impression which can become increasingly appreciated as the years pass.

When we ask young public school leavers and young

married couples whether or not they would want to make great personal sacrifice to send their own children to a public boarding school the most usual reply is a qualified 'it all depends'. Some parents, especially if they themselves are of the second or third generation to have attended a particular public school, will say that they would like their children to go to the same school as they did themselves for this special reason, that is if they were happy at school and think that the school did a good job for them. If they were unhappy or if they dislike the attitude of new headmasters or headmistresses, or if the distance from their home is too great, they may still support the public school principle and say that they would like to send their children to a similar school but not necessarily the one that they attended.

For most parents the decision will depend firstly on the income they expect to have, whom they marry or have married, the composition of their future family and, they rightly add, on what seems best at the time for any particular child. Decisions will not be on ideas of class or family tradition as much as on a practical weighing up of the possibilities on financial grounds. There is nowadays little preconceived prejudice among public school leavers against the maintained system as such, although many of them seem singularly ignorant about it. They say that they would want to take fully into account the quality and standards as they understand them of local maintained schools. Decisions about their own jobs and where they choose to live may be heavily influenced by the type of state education provided in different areas. Many, probably most, of them openly approve of comprehensive education in principle, but if the particular comprehensive school to which they would have to send their children when the time comes does not offer the standards of education and behaviour which they themselves have experienced they would be likely to make a determined effort to find a better alternative in the independent sector.

Some young ex-public school men and women today are openly biased against the public school system, feeling some embarrassment; although, for girls at least, to have attended a public school is rarely a special advantage or disadvantage of itself when seeking employment. There are signs that it is becoming the 'done thing' to have gone through the mill in the maintained schools and that those who have the advantage, real or supposed, of attending a public or other independent school will try, if anything, to conceal the fact. To discount fashion and the effect of what is considered socially 'in' at any one point of time is to be extremely rash. Parents may hang on to treasured beliefs and to values that held sway when they were young, and find that by imposing these on their own daughter 'everyone is out of step but our Jill' and that later on she suffers in consequence. When sufficient numbers of people set out consciously or unconsciously to follow certain trends they can almost without knowing it set in train a completely new way of living. When a few young parents make decisions about the future education of their children, thinking that they have done so independently of current fashions, experience often shows in the event that hundreds or even thousands of others have come to similar decisions simultaneously. New ideas, taking a hold, seen first as small clouds on the horizon, bank up into storms which totally alter former social patterns. The same set of circumstances, financial, political or whatever, will cause people to react in similar ways: with the population as a whole unaware of what is happening, a revolution takes place.

If there is a reaction on the part of young people today against an education that might be considered by some to be 'exclusive', on what criteria would parents in the future decide to send a daughter to a public school? There is no question but that they will look more critically and decide more hesitantly about public school education for their daughters than for their sons, but this has always been so. This does, however, mean that the girls' public schools—even more than boys' schools—will have to be convincingly more attractive by comparison with the maintained schools. As decisions will be greatly influenced by the type and quality, as parents see it, of the education provided in the local maintained secondary school which their child would probably be expected to attend, it may help to try first to envisage what the maintained system of the future may be like.

THE MAINTAINED SCHOOLS OF THE FUTURE

Parental decisions will be influenced greatly by development in the state system and the quality, as they see it, of the education provided in the local secondary school which their child would probably be expected to attend. The maintained system of the future is not too difficult to foresee. Schools will become bigger—not perhaps the gigantic schools of the 3,000 pupils or more which are commonplace in America, or the very large schools built in the 1950's by the then London County Council, but schools for between 1,000 and 2,000 pupils, broken down maybe into upper and lower departments. Schools of at least 1,000 pupils will be essential in most patterns of comprehensive education if they are to provide adequate sixth-form courses, and also to avoid the worst effects of narrow neighbourhood recruitment to the schools.

The larger the catchment area, the greater the chance in general of attaining a reasonable social mix.

The larger the school the more the task of the headmaster or headmistress becomes one of administration. This does not mean that pupils need be any less well looked after; all manner of devices can be introduced to make sure that individual children are not lost in the mass. But some of the personal influence of the small school is lost; the atmosphere of the big school is bound to be different, not always and not for all children necessarily better. None the less, if we have to live in a crowd later there is no harm, for some children at least—and there can be gain—in having to learn how to survive in a crowd when still young and to learn this in the comparatively protected surroundings of a school however large.

If the recommendations of the Plowden Report are adopted and the age of transfer to secondary education is eventually changed to 12 or 13, if schools in two or more separated buildings mean that in effect a change of environment takes place anyway at some age in the middle of the secondary school course, then this of itself will produce the effects of smaller school groups, but narrower age-groups, intensifying horizontal divisions by age rather than vertical family-style groupings. Just as a wide age span, say of seven or more years, can be a disadvanatge, so a narrow age span of two or three years in one separate section of a school also has disadvantages. With an age span of four to, say, six years the younger children can learn from their seniors without being so far different in age as to be a nuisance, and the senior pupils can learn to care for and be exemplars to those in the younger age groups. The middle school arrangement, discussed earlier, would seem on this criterion to give the best solution.

The sixth form is clearly about to change in nature in the

maintained schools. There may still be the distinctive academic sixth forms with one, two or three year groups, but overlaying them will be the non-academic sixth forms, common in some girls' schools now, and one-year courses after 16 which will be job-orientated, biased toward nursing or commerce, for example. Girls' schools have long ago developed general sixths, and these were commended in the Crowther Report of 1960. We now sometimes hear about 'remedial sixths' as being future features of the new large comprehensive schools. There is also the argument raging at present about bringing into the schools vocational examination courses until now confined to the further education colleges, but how far this idea will go is difficult to forecast. Those with special interests in further education or in grammar school education are likely to put up strong resistance. Traditional grammar schools regard anything other than the strictly academic post-ordinary-level sixth forms somewhat askance; they do not welcome any watering down of the academic sixths which concentrate on preparing pupils for university entrance. But the grammar schools of the maintained system are rapidly being absorbed into comprehensive systems and, as discussed in Chapter IV, the future of the direct grant grammar schools is also in doubt.

The comprehensive schools themselves are likely to be of variable attractiveness to parents. Where buildings are new, equipment (provided on capital account) can be almost lavish compared with anything that exists or is likely to exist in the independent schools. Large comprehensive schools situated in middle-class housing areas may become virtually large grammar schools, with almost all pupils staying on at school until 17 and a considerable number staying until 18. There will be every incentive for parents who live within the catchment area to choose to save their money toward helping their children later, and meanwhile to take advantage of the state education provided in a nearby school, particularly if it is new and has the usually excellent amenities of new school buildings. The good new school will attract and tend to hold good staff, and the variety of subject options for sixth-form courses is likely far to outstrip anything that an unselective independent school of 400 or 500 pupils could hope to offer. Moreover, as sixth forms build up in the large comprehensive schools in good neighbourhoods the salaries of heads and deputy heads, and the numbers and grades of posts of special responsibility under the Burnham Scale, will all automatically rise—thus providing very favourable career prospects. There will be every incentive to make the school as big as possible.

In contrast, in less favoured neighbourhoods, where a school is old or in several scattered buildings, or wherever a headmaster or headmistress is not effective (as will sometimes happen), standards will tend to fall and parents may feel inclined if they cannot move house to go to almost any lengths to get their child away into a reliable independent school whatever the expense.

SIXTH FORMS

There will certainly have to be a large measure of flexibility about sixth-form provision. For every comprehensive school to attempt to cater for every subject at sixth-form level would be impossible and, even if possible, grossly extravagant in resources. 'Rationalization', now a word in regular use in the administration of further education, may have to be applied for sixth-form work in any comprehensive system. This may seem to be a definite argument for the sixth-form college. Sixth-form colleges will come, but for how large a share of sixth-form provision and how soon in any numbers it is impossible to guess. Sixth-form colleges would appear to be a logical and inevitable consequence of all-comprehensive systems, for strong sixth-forms in every comprehensive school would seem to be too much to hope for even in the long term. There is already a good deal of co-operation about sixth-form work between neighbouring schools both in and outside the maintained system, particularly between boys' schools and girls' schools where there are gaps in teaching staff in certain subjects. There is a new and growing trend toward parents sending girls at 16 from maintained and other day schools to join sixth forms in public boarding schools; similarly, there is an increasing number of girls who attend the independent boarding schools who leave to join the sixths of maintained schools nearer home and who would be attracted to sixth-form day colleges. If substantial numbers of pupils were to leave their public boarding schools before the sixth the schools would quickly lose the greater part of their income and their strength. Equally, if the maintained comprehensive schools were to lose significant numbers of pupils to the sixth forms of the direct grant or public schools they would find building up their own sixths, which they regard of great importance, correspondingly slow and difficult. The whole problem would seem extremely hard to resolve with mutual satisfaction. However, it is exactly at sixth-form level that the greatest hope for fruitful integration between the maintained, direct grant and independent systems lies, for after 16 the bogey of selection by ability is largely laid—only those who have good academic ability normally wish to undertake a further two-year course in school.

CHANGING SCHOOL

To be able to rectify mistakes is important, and here again the existence of an independent system of education may be vital. Parents are usually reluctant to take a child away from a school in the middle of a course and they are right. Setbacks may be temporary; a child's whim must not be indulged; diagnosis is difficult. But parents are often too reluctant to admit mistakes and take action. To take a child away from a school to begin again in a new environment may be the best possible course when things are not going well, provided that the decision can be made while there is still time for a full recovery in the new school. One of the difficulties in the maintained system, or for that matter in the independent system, is to make a clean cut in time to start again. Oddly enough, to change from an independent to a maintained school midway through secondary education and vice versa when places are available seems to be easier than to change school at some half-way stage within the maintained system itself, although this can sometimes be arranged. When a child is unhappy at a large maintained day school there is much to be said for making a complete break and paying for a place at an independent school, either day or boarding. A new start may make all the difference, especially when incipient ill health or malaise has unexplicably become evident. Equally, when children are plainly unhappy at an independent school, particularly if it is a boarding school, a decision to bring them home and finish secondary education at a maintained day school can work wonders. There is normally no financial penalty attached to changing from a maintained to an independent school, but the independent schools must ask for a term's notice or fees in lieu of notice for they have to meet heavy overheads and cannot remit fees for unexpected and un-filled casual vacancies.

To allow a girl to leave school early just because she thinks she wants to is less wise. Early leaving is something very different from changing mid-course from one school to another because of failure or for some other educational or psychological reason. To leave school before gaining quali-fications which are well within capacity is a tragedy. Ad-mittedly these qualifications may be picked up later or worked for in a college of further education, but a girl who leaves school early may never come back to any formal education. Almost all girls go through a bad patch at some time in their teens when they feel that everything is against them and they want to leave school. This may be from noth-ing more than a dislike of a certain member of the staff. More often it is brought on by a girl's own psychological and physiological changes of adolescence. For able girls this will be a passing phase. Every experienced headmistress knows and recognizes this 'broody' phase; good schools have their own techniques of deliberately driving or cajoling girls through this time of despondency. Once into sixth forms, with definite objectives ahead and with the privileges of senior members of the school community, the danger is largely past and they go ahead successfully. Thus, if a mistake is thought to have been made and a change of school even contemplated, the time to do something about it is before 14 rather than at 14 or 15, and immediately after ordinary-level examinations rather than half-way through a sixth-form course.

If parents in the future find that their children are not doing as well as they should at the comprehensive school which they attend within the maintained system, they will rightly wish to search elsewhere. There must be genuine alternatives which can usually be provided only if there is a co-existing independent system. To change from one comprehensive school to another as has been said is not easy to arrange, partly because local authorities could not countenance a general exodus from an unpopular school—there are only as many school places as children to fill them if planning has been correct and the corollary of this is that every school has to have its full complement of pupils as nearly as possible from the first year of secondary education. Moreover, there is usually no clear definition about what not doing well means or how much this is because of the shortcomings of the school or of the child. Any other comprehensive school within reasonable travelling distance of the child's home which is thought to be better will, because of its good reputation, probably be already full.

The awkward parent who is prepared to create a fuss, whether at the beginning when the choice of secondary school is first being made or later when a change of school is desired, will always do best. If the parent makes enough trouble and is prepared to go direct to a member of Parliament or to the Department of Education and Science when denied a school of first choice by the local authority, the required goal is often eventually achieved. But this is almost always at the expense of the child, who cannot help but know that there has been a row. No good comes to a child who is made a special case, particularly if this receives publicity in local newspapers. Most parents anyway are loath to make this kind of trouble; if they cannot afford the fees for independent education, they tend more often to accept what they feel is inevitable, to let children go to the school allocated without more than a mild grumble and once they are there make the best of it. If the results in the event are as disappointing as they feared (which often they are not) they are as likely to blame a child's lack of ability or unwillingness to work as to think ill of the school, but the child usually leaves school at the first legal moment with consequent educational loss.

The move toward all-comprehensive secondary education in the maintained system may motivate more parents to stretch their resources to the limit to seek alternative forms of secondary education for their children for at least some part of their school life and at whatever financial sacrifice. There will undoubtedly be some movement of this kind, not only among ex-public-school parents. Its extent will depend on the quality of the maintained schools serving the area in which the parents live or the freedom they have to move house. If parents find themselves pushed about in the confines of the maintained system, they may well in exasperation look elsewhere. In particular they may prefer a girls' school for their daughters and in some areas which are going comprehensive all the maintained schools will be co-educational; they may desire the Christian education which some public schools build into the whole of the school's life as a permeating influence not restricted to Sundays and time given to lessons in religion; they may desire a specific minority denominational religious education, for example Quaker, Methodist, Christian Science only available to them at independent schools, mostly boarding schools; or a convent education for their daughters, or boarding education for its own values in the model of the public boarding schools.

Where there should be more flexibility, now that eleven-plus selection is on the way out, there is every prospect of less. One of the arguments against selection at eleven has not been so much that children are divided at too early an age into selective and non-selective groups but that, whereas those who are selected may in an urban area have a choice of schools, those who are not selected (and therefore considered to be less privileged) may have less choice as by and large they are expected to attend the unselective school nearest to their home. This school, until now, will usually have been a secondary modern school. Most local authorities have allowed freedom of choice between modern schools, and in some big cities there has been a great deal of travelling from one area to another to attend secondary modern schools. The comprehensive-school argument is that in a totally non-selective system all parents will have equal choice. This is more likely in most areas to be 'equal non-choice'.

In rural and other sparsely populated areas there is usually no real choice of maintained school anyway—there will be just one secondary school, good, middling, indifferent or downright bad. If parents are not satisfied, their only course is to seek boarding education with or without financial assistance. In the cities there will be many available schools, inevitably of widely varying quality; in practice the real choice of maintained school may not be any greater than in rural areas and if city-dwelling parents are not satisfied with the school to which their child is allocated they too have only the independent schools or, if the child is sufficiently good academically, direct grant schools where they exist to look to as alternatives. To suggest that if no such alternative were permitted then these parents will have a greater incentive to see that the local school or schools are improved is irrelevant. As local citizens they will, it is to be hoped, press for improvement, but this cannot help their own child in time although it may help others who follow. There is, for example, no way in the state system of getting rid of a weak head of a school. Parents' only safeguard is the freedom to be able to move the child to another school, as they would assuredly do if dissatisfied in the independent sector.

However altruistic parents may be in general and in their public life and expressions of opinion, when an issue concerns their own children they become understandably and rightly self-interested. The existence of an independent system of education apart from many inherent virtues is essential in a free country as a lifeboat for those who may feel that they are getting a raw deal within the state system. There will be some bad schools as there always are, some parents will be told that their children must attend them and all appeals on educational, health or other grounds against the decision of a local education authority will not always be successful. Their grounds for discontent may be real and reasonable, but none the less impossible to accept for fear of creating unmanageable precedents. If there is no alternative that the citizen's taxed income can buy, then this could mean not only compulsory education, but compulsory attendance at a particular school—in other words, direction.

DESIRE FOR BOARDING

Parents may have good reason for desiring boarding education for a daughter other than on grounds of 'need' as defined earlier. If they live busy professional lives they may feel that their children will have a more suitable environment for individual development away from home. As industrial and commercial firms amalgamate into bigger units, professional and executive staffs are increasingly expected to move house every few years sometimes from one end of the country to the other. Elderly and ailing relatives, or other illness at home, may make conditions for school children during term unsuitable; when parents hold high posts in the local education service or are elected members of local education committees children are often better not attending schools maintained by the authority they serve. Above all, parents may desire boarding education for its own sake; in particular, they may believe in the educative value of boarding education on the model of the typical English public school—with its houses integrated into school life—Cheltenham Ladies' College, Eton, Harrow, Oundle, Roedean, Rugby, Sherborne, Winchester, Wycombe Abbey to name, without prejudice, a few. They may believe in this as an ideal *model* for a school community, not for 'snob' reasons, but for genuine educative worth. Mother and daughter at home may be constantly bickering—the girl's clothes are left about untidily, her wardrobe always a shambles, she is late getting up in the morning and too late going to bed. In this situation a boarding school can work miracles; at school domestic disciplines are routine and inescapable—they become habits which are carried over on return home and the nagging disappears. This may seem an abrogation of parental responsibility, but many a deep friendship between mother and daughter which otherwise might never have formed has been sealed by enforced separation for a few months at a time during adolescence—friendship over and above the ties of maternal and filial love. And there are the letters: a daughter (but rarely a son) will pour out all manner of intimacies, usually at great length and with increasing fluency, in letters written home from school, which face-to-face she might feel shy to reveal. No girls' boarding school need worry about 'free-style' writing—the essays are written all right, on Sundays, spelling mistakes and all; valuable for both the girls and their parents, that is until the day comes when after-six telephone calls home, with all their fearful emotional frustrations, may be allowed in lieu.

Boarding education on this model would seem to be every bit as much a legitimate 'wish' of parents for their children in the meaning of the 1944 Education Act as denominational or single-sex education. Indeed, the wish may be for all three and ideally combined in a girls' public boarding school. The state does not and indeed cannot imaginably have the money to provide or subsidize boarding education for the whole of secondary education to meet parents' mere desire as opposed to serious 'need' (nursery education, a far less expensive item, would be years ahead of boarding in any national priorities), but, as the desire is reasonable, if parents are prepared to pay, it would be unthinkable in a democratic country to deny them the opportunity or to create a situation in which independent schools of their choice could not exist. Similarly, if parents seek a boarding convent education for their daughters, whether they are themselves Roman Catholic or Anglican or not, provided they are prepared to pay any necessary fees, they cannot reasonably be denied their wishes.

The argument so far has not involved selection by ability and presumably there is no conflict about the principle of allowing independent fee-paying boarding schools to exist— indeed, the terms of reference of the Commission presuppose that they will continue, albeit with some different method of recruiting pupils. The conflict arises in that the public boarding schools also, by definition, have good sixth forms and so to some extent select by academic ability. But what is the alternative? Parents desiring this kind of boarding education for a daughter may also reasonably wish her to have the same opportunity of an extended academic education as is promised in maintained comprehensive schools. It has already been argued that no secondary school of fewer than about a thousand pupils with recruitment from a full cross-section of ability can expect to have viable sixth forms. Only one girls' public boarding school, Cheltenham Ladies' College with 822 girls, has more than 800 pupils of secondary school age—the majority have places for fewer than 400. Few, if any, have the resources to increase boarding accommodation even marginally, let alone double or treble it without some help from public funds. Moreover, a large school of 1,200 or more pupils (the accepted minimum size normally now for a fully comprehensive school in the maintained system) would mean a type of boarding education not necessarily best for girls of 13 or 14—the 'model' that is sought for girls' boarding schools may preclude large schools even if there were a practical possibility of providing them, which there is not. The logic seems plain: if a boarding school for girls is to be of socially and educationally convenient size, say, for between 200 and 800 girls, and yet provide strong (or even merely viable) academic sixth forms, it *has* to be selective. This does not mean that all independent schools must or should select only from the top half of the ability range—they do not—but there must be the possibility, indeed a policy, of selection within certain defined ability brackets for some girls' boarding schools if all pupils in these relatively small schools are to have a curriculum suited to their aptitudes and abilities and if each school is to be well staffed and yet run economically. This argument is purely educational and has nothing to do with other valued aspects of independence, in particular the *right* of an independent school to select, that is to choose the pupils it recruits, and the right to refuse or reject unsuitable applicants.

Parents will take all factors into account before deciding to educate their daughters outside the state system. They will naturally be much influenced in their choice of school for their children by what they envisage to be their likely eventual careers. If the goal is for the children to go to a university, but the local comprehensive school appears not to provide good enough academic courses this will be a strong argument in favour of paying fees to get what is wanted. Considerations for girls will often be different from those for boys and the weight given to career prospects much less. Graduate mothers will almost always insist where possible that their daughters stay on in full-time education until at least 17; they do not necessarily think that because they went to a university themselves their own daughters must be pushed into doing the same, but they do understand what a university course entails for a girl, and they may feel strongly that a public boarding school, or at least one or two years away from home, may be a good preparation for university. A girl who has never been away from home and who is suddenly plunged into the rough and tumble of university or college life, often in inadequate lodgings, has huge adjustments to make. The girl who has been to a boarding school or who has had a year between school and college in some form of employment which involves being away from home has a big advantage during the first year of residential higher education. Parents, particularly mothers, who themselves have had a university education are well aware of this.

Choosing the best school for a son or daughter is a responsibility and problem that all parents have to face, and have always had to face if they have cared enough and if there is genuine choice, whether they are confined to the state system for the education of their children or have sufficient income to be able to choose whether or not to send them to independent schools. Children differ widely even within one family, but each child has only one life to live;

parents cannot wait for schools to change or improve although their influence can help them to do so. Moreover schools, whether maintained or independent, alter in character and standards from one generation to another in any event. Parents' own school experience is often a misleading guide about what is best for their children. The best that parents can hope to do is to make themselves as well acquainted as possible with what is going on around them in education and to keep in touch without any extensive break with schools which they and their friends know well and with trends in local schools. We learn best from meeting pupils still at school and from those who have just left and by taking every opportunity possible of visiting schools.

FINANCIAL CONSIDERATIONS

The eventual decision about where to send a child to school may depend very much on financial circumstances. Even when young parents can assess their future income and the demands likely to be made on it in any way accurately, the decisions are anything but simple. The most common device for paying for public school education, now that grandparents' gifts are drying up, is through insurance savings policies—the education being paid for in effect from the time of the child's birth irrespective of which secondary school is eventually chosen. But fewer parents of young children these days can save in this way: many of them are already mortgaged to the hilt in trying to buy their houses. The trend toward having larger families, partly itself a consequence of earlier marriage, is also likely to have profound effects on parents' ability to send any of their children to public boarding schools. Few parents wish to distinguish between their children in the amount they spend on them. Some will be willing to make sacrifices to help pay for the education of a son rather than for a daughter, but this is usually only because they expect and are prepared to have to contribute towards a girl's expenses (even after her marriage) long after they expect to have to do so for a wage-earning or salary-earning son. If there are four children in a family, public boarding school education other than on scholarships tends to be automatically ruled out, even for professional families with what can or could once be regarded as high incomes. Many parents in the past, if not in this new generation, limited the size of their families for this one principal reason of enabling them to educate the children they had at fee-paying schools of their choice. It seems unreasonable to condemn this restraint.

When the children have arrived, even when there are no more than two, there is still the question of the second car or, if the husband has a car paid for by his employers, the car for family use. The capital and running cost of a car is roughly the same as the cost of educating a child at a private preparatory school followed by a public boarding school. The second car is no longer a matter for many families merely of luxury and convenience. For the wife to have the regular use of a car on weekdays may be as essential to the good education of young children as understood by these parents as is any saving for expenditure on independent education later on. Indeed, not merely as essential, often more essential. Parents may feel that pre-school education before the age of 5 is of great importance. In this they are right, but state nursery school provision, as has been said, is inadequate and in many areas virtually non-existent. The mother then needs a car to take a 4-year-old, for example, to a private nursery school, if the baby is to be safely cared for.

Public transport is hopelessly poor in many suburban as well as rural and semi-rural areas. Married women can come back to teaching or to other professional or social work for which they have been trained much more easily if they have the use of a car for travelling to and from work, for shopping and for transporting their own children to and from school. Visits to the dentist, to music lessons, to grandparents and to the countryside—which are nowadays often possible only when there is a car for family use—may be considered as important for the children's general education and well-being as any particular choice of school, provided that the state schools available are at least reasonably reliable.

The possession of the second car radically alters decisions about private nursery education and preparatory schools—acting partly in their favour. The distance from home to school no longer makes as much difference—three miles travelling or five is little more deterrent than half a mile. Once the routine is established of taking and fetching children when they are still at the very beginning of their school years, the habit can easily be extended to last through the whole of the primary or preparatory stage.

If parental income is sufficient to have a car purely for family use and to be able to contemplate public school education as well, this then becomes of relevance to decisions not only about whether or not to send children to a public school, but which public school to choose. When cars were rarer and the second car was the prerogative of the chauffeur-employing parent, a long-distance train journey was accepted as a part of public boarding school education. The distance of the school from the home made little difference to the decisions. Parents rarely visited more than once a term; often only one term in a year. Boarders seldom had home leave at half-term, let alone at other week-ends, however near they lived. Now, with rail fares high and the family car the normal form of transport, parents are much *more* influenced by the travelling distance to the school, preferring the relatively short rather than the long drive. The advantage lies also increasingly with those schools within easy reach of London, in attracting pupils—and, even more important, in recruiting and holding staff. Other schools find that they recruit pupils mostly from towns and country areas within easy driving distance and that they become increasingly dependent on part-time women graduate staff who live within daily driving distance from the school. The possession of a family car and the tendency to choose a school within easy driving distance affects attitudes toward visiting week-ends, half-term home leave and weekly boarding—all of which are more common now than a generation ago.

With ever higher taxation, particularly on unearned incomes, paying fees for public boarding education is becoming an increasingly daunting proposition for professional parents. Although waiting lists for the leading girls' public schools are still full, there are signs that whenever fees have to be raised, for example to meet new salary awards for teachers, names are withdrawn. There is little reserve of parental income remaining. The schools cannot risk raising fees faster than incomes rise—and yet if they do not they will find difficulty in keeping up the standards of the education and amenities they offer.

The first choice to be made by parents who seek independent education for a daughter is between day and boarding. Where parents live in the vicinity of a girls' public day school, there will be a strong incentive to attempt to gain a place for her there. Competition to get into these schools is intense—comparable to that of gaining a place at a direct grant grammar school; there may be from four to ten times as many applicants as places and hitherto these schools have selected in the main on academic ability. Whether this will always be so depends in part on the recommendations of the Public Schools Commission and any government decisions then made. If the girl cannot gain a place the next choice for parents must be among the public boarding schools or other independent day or boarding schools. Some of the girls' public boarding schools recruit from a wider ability range than the large girls' public day schools and they make their entrance requirements flexible enough to help girls' whose primary or preparatory education has not been markedly good. The independent schools taken all together probably provide for the full range of ability according to demand. There are many small independent schools for girls in the suburban and dormitory areas of large towns and cities, daygirls, boarders and sometimes for both, which have specialized for years in accepting 'eleven-plus failures' and bringing them up to GCE standards. Their usefulness may still be great even when there is no eleven-plus and comprehensive schools set out to fulfil this same function.

If, however, the aim of parents is to send their daughter to a public boarding school how will they decide which school to choose? Having made up their minds how much they can afford in fees and travel, and having ruled out those schools that are too distant or too expensive, they will probably weigh the following considerations, not necessarily in this order:

(i) their own 'old school' if ex-public school;
(ii) their denominational allegiance, if any;
(iii) other personal connections, if any, and whether

friends, relatives or neighbours have or have had
daughters at the school;

(iv) the school's reputation, particularly in academic
achievement or in any other field in which the child
shows promise;

(v) their impression of the headmistress and the quality
of the staff;

(vi) convenience of the school's location as regards travelling (but not necessarily within too easy reach of
home);

(vii) the size, organization, educational and recreational
facilities of the school;

(viii) the attraction of the school buildings, its amenities
and surroundings;

(ix) general considerations, including social and moral
attitudes and, above all, the ethos of the school.

Wise parents will visit not one but several schools before
finally making up their minds. They do well to begin making
visits when they first think that a public boarding school
may offer the education they would most wish for a daughter,
perhaps putting her name down for more than one school
and then revisiting again about a year or two before she
would be first entering. The girls' public schools offer a fine
education. Even if radical change is forced upon them they
can still remain good schools. Parents who can afford to
send a daughter to a public school and decide to do so will
have no regrets.

CHAPTER EIGHT

The Future of the Girls' Schools

'INTEGRATION'

The girls' public schools, with their fairly wide recruitment across the ability range and their flexible traditions, would appear to be more favourably placed to adjust and to collaborate with the state system than are some of the older boys' foundations.

The girls' schools have always been more democratic than the boys' in their professional structure, partly because they came later in history. The Governing Bodies of Girls' Schools Association (GBGSA) admits schools with probably a wider academic intake than the boys' Governing Bodies' Association; the Association of Head Mistresses (AHM) is open to headmistresses of all recognized secondary schools whether independent, direct grant or maintained by local authorities and has about a thousand members from all types of secondary school, large and small, urban and rural, and, through overseas membership, schools of multi-racial composition; the Association of Headmistresses of Boarding Schools (AHMBS) with 140 members likewise covers a wide range of schools, in size, in the academic range of their pupils and in the proportion of daygirls to boarders. Headmistresses and assistant staff of the girls' public schools are constantly meeting colleagues from all types of schools in their professional organizations.

The girls' public schools cover a wide social range. Some of them were 'charity' schools, some were founded to provide an education for the daughters of 'gentlemen engaged in the professions', for example, or of clergymen, or of 'warehouse-men and clerks'. The foundress of one Catholic Order established three types of schools—first, schools for the poor, then schools for girls from middle class homes and finally schools for the wealthy, and these three groups of schools were very distinct from 1820 until recent years, the schools originally founded for the wealthy being those which have remained independent. Gradually these distinctions have blurred—they were in their time as much taken for granted as today they are looked at askance. Few girls' independent day schools would nowadays feel that there is any *social* exclusiveness in their intake of girls—particularly is this so of the direct grant schools. Most independent boarding schools are necessarily socially weighted towards girls whose parents can afford and wish to pay boarding and tuition fees, but most of the schools would welcome a more socially mixed intake if some way of finding the fees for girls from less well-off homes can be found. The public schools usually arrange headmistresses' salaries privately; house mistresses and other resident staff may also receive salaries which are specially negotiated. Even so, the girls' public schools, particularly boarding schools in rural areas, have the same difficulties about recruiting well-qualified women teaching staff as any other girls' schools, but they have had a tradition for many years of employing women graduates part time. There is a good deal of flexibility in a boarding school for both the school and part-time staff in arranging the working week, and the girls, especially those in sixth forms, are able to benefit by this. The independent schools are not subject to the quota of full-time teachers laid down annually for local authorities by the Secretary of State, but there is no evidence to suggest that, when allowances are made for sixth-form work and/or boarding duties and for music staff, they are more generously staffed than maintained schools. Furthermore, most teachers who take up posts in independent schools, particularly boarding schools, usually do so by deliberate choice and would not necessarily continue in teaching if the schools lost their independent status.

In their own way the girls' schools sometimes feel that they have even more to lose than the boys' schools. Their independence and recognition has been hardly fought for; the risks they took in the early pioneering days of the end of the last century inured them to living on a knife edge of financial uncertainty and yet winning through. Courage has been their hallmark. Glad, indeed anxious, as they may be to co-operate and to make their contribution to the national and local systems of education they are united in their unwillingness to knuckle under to any outside dictation, least of all to threats from politicians. If any group of people are going to shout that the emperor has no clothes and blow to bits any new theories of education if these seem unsound or of doubtful value it will be the headmistresses of the girls' schools.

The Governing Bodies of Girls' Schools Association recently formulated six principles on which the girls' independent public schools might wish to stand firm in any discussions about integration.

1. The retention of an independent governing body, by which is meant an autonomous body with an independent chairman.

2. The freedom to maintain the religious tradition of the school.
3. The retention of the financial control of the school, including the freedom to allocate the income of the school.
4. The freedom to appoint the headmistress and staff and to decide their conditions of appointment.
5. The freedom to decide the curriculum.
6. The freedom to admit and retain only those pupils capable of benefiting by the education offered.

The schools feel strongly about the independence of their governing bodies, but most schools would welcome as members representatives from local authorities. Governors of direct grant schools would agree that local authority members bring useful experience and knowledge, and they help to provide a link between the schools and the local education service.

Freedom to maintain the religious tradition of the school would seem an unarguable right. Retention of financial control means in practice ensuring that the school remains solvent. Independent schools are not restricted about the amount of money they spend on buildings, for example, or in the way that they allocate their income under different heads of expenditure. Far from this leading to luxury spending, it more usually means, at least for the girls' schools, a most carefully considered economy of resources in the continual effort to keep costs to a minimum without damaging educational standards. The independent schools have to give value for money if they are to survive, and they need freedom to manage their own budgets if they are to do this to best advantage.

Freedom to appoint the headmistress and staff is all-important. The quality of any school depends on the head, and the headmistress of an independent school, with her almost complete autonomy, will control the whole tone of the school. Unlike the head of a maintained school she is the principal 'recruiting officer' as well as as the academic and administrative head. She receives parents, and whether or not parents decide to send their daughters to the school is very much influenced by their impression of her. The governors must therefore have the right to negotiate her salary—they also must retain the right to ask her for her resignation if they are not satisfied with her stewardship. The independent schools are not bound by Burnham scales for teachers' salaries. The public schools probably all pay up to Burnham for full-time staff—otherwise they would be without teachers, but few, if any, girls' public schools can afford to pay above Burnham scales. They do have the advantage, in having freedom to decide conditions of appointment, of being able to make special arrangements with teachers about time out of school, free days, leave of absence for special reasons, and independent schools can be flexible about the choice of dates for school holidays. Freedom to decide the curriculum and to admit and retain only those pupils capable of benefiting by the education offered would seem to rule out any insistence on a school recruiting pupils from a full range of ability unless it feels itself equipped to give them all a suitable education. Very few of the girls' public schools are large enough to be able to contemplate accepting girls without regard to ability for the full secondary school course, or to be able to do equally well for the ablest girls and the least able simultaneously. Many of them do, however, take girls with only average academic potential and they might well be prepared to accept more from the lower brackets of academic ability. Some of the girls' public schools now take more girls from the middle than the top brackets and some accept girls of only modest academic ability who have other attributes, for example, a talent for music. All independent girls' boarding schools taken as a whole do probably cater for the full range of ability and, as the Alexander report on Boarding Education showed, collectively they could probably provide for all girls who are judged to be in 'need' of boarding education.

COLLABORATION

There is a good deal of collaboration between public and maintained schools. Oundle since its foundation has accepted all boys from Laxton Grammar School who qualify for a sixth-form course; Dauntsey's in Wiltshire has a close connection with a local secondary modern school. Similar forms of collaboration between girls' schools have already been mentioned.

The independent schools cannot and must not expect that 'integration' would bring a large influx of pupils who are all from the top ability brackets and paid for from public funds. This would be to contravene the whole principle of no-selection-by-ability to different schools which is the *sine qua non* of comprehensive reorganization. Sixth-form recruitment does to some extent take care of this, because pupils who stay on into sixth forms voluntarily are self-selected by this criterion alone. How far the public schools would be prepared to recruit to their sixth forms only, on top of their own intake of pupils who had come to the schools at the normal ages of 11, 12 or 13, is problematical. Some 25 per cent of new intake direct to the sixth might be acceptable to some schools, but not to others unless the whole character of the schools were to be radically altered. More than 25 per cent would probably be ruled out by most schools. No one has yet given any clear picture of what the education for the younger pupils in a school would be like if there were an overwhelming proportion of sixth-formers, many of whom had not themselves come up through the lower forms of the school. We know that a relatively small number of newcomers to the sixths are a great asset to a school and add to the richness of the work and social experience of all pupils—and, incidentally, of the staff—but so far we have no experience of a really 'top-heavy' school and few would wish to plunge into this sort of formation on a large scale without a period of trial. The Public Schools Commission may recommend just such an experiment—several schools might then be willing to start modestly and allow the pattern to grow as they learnt from experience.

There may be sound reasons for choosing a few selected schools which have outstanding reputations for teaching mathematics and the physical sciences to develop these subjects in new ways for specially talented boys and girls. The Russians do this. There is a serious educational case here to be examined; pupils who show outstanding gifts in these subjects would be able to go, publicly supported and with scholarships, to these schools. They would follow a wide curriculum, but with the sure knowledge that they would come in contact with specially gifted (and rare) teachers of high mathematical ability. We tend to fight shy of this kind of highlighting of special abilities in the young—certainly this idea cuts right across the grain of British Socialist thinking about comprehensive education.

Where a school has some special line in modern languages or in some rare language—Russian or even Chinese—which we can never hope to provide in more than a few of our maintained secondary schools, there could be real advantage in this being strongly developed and for pupils who have shown language talent at an early age at their local school to be allowed to transfer. A public boarding school could make a house wholly French-speaking, for example, and this could give a great spurt to pupils' competence in language.

Some schools, too, which already have a reputation for providing exceptionally well for certain special aptitudes—music, art, preparation for careers in medicine or agriculture, for example—might well be happy to develop these special biases more strongly and offer places for pupils from local authorities which may find this kind of provision difficult to make. The girls' schools have never allowed early specialization although some may have concentrated overmuch on academic subjects. In general, we need later and less specialization rather than more in our secondary schools, but this may be precisely a reason for giving a wide spread of subjects in all schools until after the age of 16 and leaving relatively few schools to produce the special courses at sixth-form level.

At the age of entry to secondary education most girls' public schools have a good deal of flexibility about the required academic attainments and, over the years, they have shown great willingness to adjust and compromise to suit the needs of girls who may have had very varied primary or preparatory school education. The age of entry, too, is usually flexible, with girls coming in to junior departments where these exist at almost any age for which the school may cater. Senior schools recruit usually at either 11 or 13, but again girls may join the school at almost any age thereafter whenever there are vacancies. When girls go to boarding schools before 13, and especially if before 11, this is almost always to junior departments of schools, mostly small, which provide both primary and secondary education with one continuous curriculum. With the reorganization of maintained schools to form systems of secondary education which may have a break between separated buildings, if not between schools, at about 13, and with the possibility of several comprehensive schemes incorporating 'middle schools' with transfer to the senior schools at 12, 13 or even 14, the girls' public schools may decide to recruit only at 12 or later. There should be little or no difficulty in co-ordinating curricula broadly between the girls' independent and maintained schools. Different contributions might be made by independent schools in different areas and there is no reason why the schools should not negotiate with local authorities separately within their own or neighbouring areas and make what arrangements they may think fit and that best suit their several circumstances—after all, is this not what independence implies?

FINANCE

The public schools, like all independent schools, are facing grave financial difficulties. Most of the public schools are old foundations (Table iv), some with buildings centuries old still in use. These buildings might have to be extensively modified and added to if the schools are to accept pupils on a wider academic basis. Some schools have new modern boarding houses, new sixth-form studies, laboratories, gymnasia and swimming pools; but many of the schools are still housed in old premises at least in part, solid maybe, perhaps too indestructible, but costly to maintain, inconvenient, inadequately heated and with rooms often the wrong shape or size for modern ideas about education, the whole disastrously difficult and expensive to run. No amount of economy and use of pupil-labour in domestic chores can overcome these basic practical handicaps. If there is no change in their status, rising costs are bound to force up fees. Left to themselves, how are these schools to stay in the race?

The main and often only financial asset of a number of the public schools, girls' as well as boys' schools, is their sites. Where the schools are in or near urban areas or in designated development areas, a few may be able to sell ground or parts of their buildings most advantageously. The suggestion has been made several times recently that one way for some of the public schools to integrate with the maintained sector would be to offer parts of their sites or their playing fields to their local authority to build comprehensive day schools, the existing independent school then becoming part of a campus, either as a boarding annex for all secondary age groups, or as a sixth-form college. This, indeed, would be integration in a big way. Would the schools then be able to retain their independence? How far would they be willing or, indeed, able to go? If any land or property they own is redundant to their educational needs, they would most likely feel that they would have to be hardheaded and sell in the open market. A compulsory purchase order clamped on a school by a local authority for school building purposes would be a sure way of destroying goodwill. Moreover, to sell any part of a school itself (other than land or outlying property) might seriously diminish the school's attractiveness and amenities and even the number of pupils whom it could accept, which would then bring down potential income.

Some public schools with junior houses may consider selling these to increase their capital resources. Girls' schools in particular may find this a good policy, although in some ways the existence of junior departments may have formed the strongest pull for the girls' schools in attracting pupils. Any device of this kind can only be of short-term value (even if itself desirable and wise) in solving the long-term problem of survival in what may be a continuingly and increasingly difficult financial situation.

Most of the public schools are too small rather than too large to be financially and educationally soundly based and their best policy ideally would lie not in selling land even if there is any to spare but in building themselves. This, for the schools, is the rub. From where are they to obtain capital for any large-scale building? Only a few have spare capital assets and many of the rest have already taken out mortgages on existing buildings for capital expenditure on improvements and necessary repairs.

Almost the only source of new capital for most of the public and direct grant schools is through appeals. Covenants whereby tax at standard rate is recovered by the recipient charities on annual gifts over a covenanted period of at least seven years are the most effective help in appeals.

In general, industry and commerce are slow to respond to appeals for schools, although the Industrial Fund for the Advancement of Science (now closed) gave vital assistance to the independent schools in providing laboratories. Most schools have to depend entirely on their alumni and on parents for support for appeals. The girls' schools have a much more difficult task than the boys' schools, largely because, at least until recent years, women in Great Britain (in contrast to American women) do not own a significant share of available capital wealth.

There is a good deal of misunderstanding about tax remission in respect of gifts to charities and insurance policies. The public schools, as charities, are relieved from the selective employment tax and are entitled to 50 per cent mandatory relief from rates, and grandparents can assist with the cost of education by covenanted gifts to individual children, but the amount contributed in this way is small compared with the total of all fees paid and it is decreasing. It has not been possible for many years in this country to set gifts to charities against income before assessment for surtax and, since the Finance Act of 1965, covenanted gifts to individuals have also been excluded from this relief. Nor, since the introduction of Corporation Tax in 1965, have companies been able to set against profit for tax purposes contributions toward the school fees of children of employees. Likewise, industrial trust funds for educational or charitable purposes can no longer earn remission of tax—a case in the High Court in 1966 established this beyond doubt.

At no time have parents been able to benefit in tax relief by any scheme relating to their own children's school fees. Annuities taken out by a father on his life for payment during a child's school years produce a small concession, equivalent to two-fifths of the premium, against income tax (as do other life insurance policies), but none against surtax, and this concession is restricted in accordance with income levels.

There is strong feeling about tax relief, because it is a form of central or local government subsidy. But the total loss to the Exchequer in revenue from tax is very small indeed compared with the amount of money saved to public funds through not having to provide free education for the children who now attend the independent schools. The 1966–67 'out-county' rates of payment between local authorities are £130 a year for pupils of 11 to 15 and £260 for pupils of 16 and over. In 1965 there were 152,232 boys and girls aged 11 to 15 and 46,422 aged 16 and over in independent day and boarding schools recognized as efficient in England and Wales. The cost of educating them in maintained schools would thus have been £35 million a year without taking any account of the capital cost of school buildings or of boarding accommodation or boarding charges.

Perhaps the greatest contribution that a benevolent Government could make to help the public schools would be to allow legacies to educational institutions and other named charities to be free of death duty. In America duty-free legacies and exemption even from standard income tax on gifts to charities up to 10 per cent of personal income are most important sources of income for their famous privately endowed colleges, universities, research institutions and art galleries.

All ideas about integration presuppose some suitable financial arrangements as regards fees and revenue expenditure. The Fleming idea of sponsored places on a direct grant principle failed, and there seems no real prospect of the idea succeeding in the even harsher economic climate of today. Nor is the Department of Education and Science likely to agree to put aside money for backing any scheme to send pupils to public schools unless in doing so there is a clear financial saving in some compensating direction. The Royal Commission on Local Government is at present considering the reorganization of local government and may recommend a structure of, say, some forty regions or provinces in a 'first tier' and boroughs in a 'second tier' covering a population of not less than 250,000 people. The regions rather than the boroughs might more easily co-ordinate and pay for pupils in the public and direct grant schools and sponsor boarding education where 'need' could be established. The second tier, that is the boroughs of comparable size to the existing large local authorities, would however almost certainly be given the responsibility for most if not all secondary education. Nothing happening now in large county boroughs can lead anyone to hope that attitudes would be any more generous in new boroughs in the future than in local education authorities now toward paying for pupils in independent schools on a direct-grant or other subsidizing principle.

There is a half-way measure, called 'pooling', whereby local authorities meet the cost of providing a service collectively. This perhaps gives the greatest hope as machinery for assisting parents with boarding school fees on a sliding scale according to income. The Department of Education and Science in this way would be relieved of the necessity to increase their Vote, except in so far as they may be persuaded to subsidize the central pool fund. Local authorities do not have a separate item in their budgets showing how much they have paid for the pupils whom they themselves have sponsored, but the item shows retrospectively as the authority's share of the total cost incurred by all local authorities for all pupils sponsored through the pool. For example, the total number of pupils recommended to all the schools by all the local authorities might be 2,000. The total cost for the 2,000 for that year would then be divided between all the authorities according to a formula based on population or other relevant factors suitably weighted; the amount paid by any one authority is not dictated by the number sent by that authority.

This works well from the point of view of the receiving schools, although it is anathema to most county and county borough treasurers, who not unjustifiably regard pooling as the end of purposive financial responsibility. Members of local education committees tend to feel that, as they will have to pay a share in any event, they may as well take advantage of the scheme and they nominate pupils with an abandon they would not contemplate if their finance committee could take them to task over the full real expenditure. The costs of a scheme need not be met in total through the pool. Parents could still be required to meet all or part of the tuition and/or boarding fees according to their incomes. The central government if so minded could make a contribution to the pool and could also make some arrangement about advancing capital to the schools for building purposes at favourable rates as is now done for aided schools, or even make grants toward the costs necessarily incurred by the schools in building to meet any large new demands on accommodation for the purpose of collaborating with local authorities.

The training of teachers is financed through a local authority pool; so are advanced courses in colleges of further education. The education of the small number of 'no-authority' pupils and students whose parents are abroad and have no residential qualification is financed through a pooling arrangement, as also is the Further Education Staff College where lecturers and other staff from colleges of further education attend for short courses. Pooling is a cunning device that has worked well in assisting the development of advanced courses in further education and helped the colleges of advanced technology on the way to direct grant status and thence to full university charters. It provides an easily understood rough justice when applied to the training of teachers. It does not, however, tend to find favour with those local authorities who discover that they seem always to be paying for facilities outside their boundaries which they may feel they might prefer to provide themselves and over which they have no direct financial control. Whether the local authority associations (as they exist now or as they may become under any future reorganization of local government) would be willing to operate a scheme of this kind in order to send significant numbers of pupils to public schools is another matter—my experience as an elected member of a local authority would lead me to doubt it. Whatever the machinery, the cost to public funds is the same. If 25 per cent of secondary school places in independent recognized schools were taken up by local authorities, the cost would be at least £9 million without regard to boarding. Surely we would feel that nursery education, for example, should have a higher priority than fussing about the public schools?

There is one completely different solution which is being mooted—coupons or vouchers. Parents would be given vouchers representing the cost of primary and secondary education in the maintained schools over the span of compulsory schooling. They would then be free to use these coupons either in maintained schools without further expenditure or to use them as part-payment of fees at other schools adding from their own pockets any additional costs. The vouchers would count as income and be subject to normal income tax and surtax, and therefore would not give the same financial advantage to those who opt out of the state system as any scheme for straight tax relief on the cost of education *not* taken up in maintained schools.

The idea of vouchers is to increase parents' range of choice of schools, to give more parents the opportunity for choice, and, by encouraging more parents to pay part of the cost of educating their children, to reduce by that amount the general taxation on all citizens. We are almost certainly too committed to the welfare state to attempt to put the clock back in this way and most people in government, whether national or local, would flatly reject the voucher idea as not being a practical proposition. Whatever its merits may appear to be in theory, it would be considered a political non-starter however strongly its advocates feel otherwise—and the concern of Government of whatever political colour must be with real possibilities within a foreseeable future.

THE LONG-TERM FUTURE

Never has the future as far as the independent schools are concerned been more difficult to foretell. The leading public schools will almost certainly continue in some form or another—they are too good to founder entirely. But the times are changing and, apart from any threatened political action, unless the schools are flexible enough to change too they may, as some people hope they will, gradually be swept away by the tide of advance of full-subsidized state education. The remarkable story of progress since the war in the maintained system is and should be a source of considerable civic pride. Not only in buildings and in sheer numbers of pupils and students has there been a revolution, but in ideas about how children learn, about what to teach and how to teach it. This applies for children of low ability as well as for the high-flyers, and over all age groups. The resources of the state have been available to encourage research and improvement. Although research used to be minimal and opportunities for exploiting new ideas within the maintained schools sporadic and chancy, the situation as it has recently developed is radically different and far more favourable to change and fruitful experimentation. This is good from every point of view.

Experiment and change have not been confined to the maintained schools. New ideas and developments have come equally from the independent sector. Sevenoaks and A. S. Neill's Summerhill are, in fact, better known in America than to most British people. The public schools were themselves a great innovation at the time of their foundation and the younger public schools have each in turn almost all had some special new ideas or contributions to bring, just as the new universities have now brought fresh ideas to higher education. Long-established public schools have been quick to embrace and help, for example, in the Nuffield Science Project and in the several new mathematics projects—in at least as great degree as the maintained schools. With their well-qualified graduate staffs they are able to pioneer new academic courses as well as continuing traditional studies where they see fit.

The jolt likely to be caused in the state system by proposed reorganization into all-comprehensive education, in some areas alarmingly precipitate and too-hastily planned, may bring some setbacks. The sudden cessation of maintained grammar schools in their modern post-war form is sure for the time being to mean some loss of power in sixth-form development. But no one closely in touch with state education believes that the momentum of progress will now be curbed for long even by the disruptions of reorganization. Directions may change: there will almost certainly here and there be fierce and bitter arguments which may leave deep scars, many of which need not have been inflicted. But in ten or twenty years' time these will have disappeared and the general picture should again be of dramatic total advance.

Higher standards in the maintained system are not achieved cheaply either in money, effort or manpower. The 'out-county' payment for a pupil in a sixth form today between one local authority and another, as has already been said, is now £260 a year and constantly being raised. This includes a small element for administration, school health and loan charges, but is for day education only and there is nothing for food or boarding in this amount. This is a measure of the competition which the independent schools, entirely unsubsidized, are up against. If we reckon that boarding costs £200 per pupil, this means that boarding school sixth-form fees would have to be at least £460 to match maintained standards of provision. Only seven girls' schools in the country have fees of over £500 and the fees at most girls' independent boarding schools are very much lower.

For all the fine progress in the maintained schools, the independent schools have increased in usefulness. They have their own ethos and they provide at the moment the only significant amount of boarding education, particularly for academically able pupils. Moreover, in a free society there must be room for the eccentric. We do not have to send our own children to a 'way-out' school if we do not wish to do so, but, provided that there is such guarantee against scandalous institutions as exists under the 1944 Act, most of us would defend to the last ditch the right for them to exist.

In all the discussions about integration, about this or that percentage of places at public schools 'to be allotted to pupils from maintained schools assisted from public funds on a scale related to parental income', no one has yet come forward with any suggestion that holds water about how to choose the pupils—other than on grounds of boarding 'need' and/or sixth-form courses in special subjects when these are not available in local comprehensive schools. The first group of parents to benefit by any scheme of the 'Fleming type' would be the middle-class parents who would most desire this kind of education—those same ex-public school parents who are now sending their children to maintained schools because they cannot afford fees. The child from the deprived or the broken home is usually best at a small boarding school within easy reach of the parent who has custody—not at a public boarding school. No one can seriously suggest that the nation would be helped by turning the public boarding schools wholly or mainly into schools for those in need of boarding education even if the cost of this could be seriously contemplated.

The public day schools have not even this reason for being used as schools for those with special needs other than the desire for high academic standards—their case is strictly akin to that of the direct grant day schools.

The future of the public schools depends a good deal on political pressures and what happens in the next and subsequent general elections. The two main political parties have fundamentally different approaches to the public schools. A future Conservative Government would be likely to leave the public schools to work out their own salvation, considering duty-free legacies perhaps and a central pool for helping parents with fees and allowing, maybe, as much encouragement as possible to local authorities to take up places in the public schools to meet special needs and, in particular, to take a more generous view of what is regarded as constituting boarding 'need'. But they would be unlikely to do more than this. Conservatives are very sensitive to any accusation of using public funds to establish privilege for those who already have social advantages. As public money is always likely to be short and the demands of the state system of education, including the universities, seem to be insatiable, Conservatives will probably continue to prefer to concentrate on raising standards in the maintained schools rather than on subsidizing independent education other than marginally. Conservative opinion is not convinced that the public schools are such a divisive influence in society as Labour chooses to make them out to be, nor, in so far as they are socially divisive, are Conservatives convinced that this has such dire effects on society as is supposed.

Labour, in contrast, is politically committed to 'doing something about the public schools'. Their leaders may be content enough that there should *appear* to be something being done—and setting up the Public Schools Commission does for the time being suppress adverse comment from the more left-wing supporters about not keeping to electoral promises. If Labour remains in power for a considerable time, say for eight or ten years more, big changes are sure to have taken place—partly because almost all maintained secondary schools would by the late 1970's have been reorganized into one or other comprehensive arrangement. The public and direct grant schools can hardly be permitted under Labour to co-exist indefinitely in their present essentially selective form alongside a wholly non-selective state system.

Mr Anthony Crosland has publicly stated that he has no intention of making the payment of fees for private education illegal. No responsible government in this country could seriously suggest this. Not only would it be an unacceptable infringement of individual freedom, but there would always have to be exceptions to uniformity even apart from schools for the handicapped. Nothing as drastic as that would be required to eliminate most of the public schools in their present form. Any ill-intentioned government could quickly bring them to their knees without specific legislation. A government would only need to withdraw the concession of paying only half rates as charities and many of the independent schools would quickly have to throw in their hands. To make a selective employment tax apply to independent schools, as has now happened to those not registered as charities, would also put an intolerable burden on many of them already operating on tiny margins. To curtail covenanting for annual donations to capital funds would sink some schools. Any government which set out to get rid of the public schools would find this easy enough.

In any event, most of the leading public schools want to co-operate in some way with the state system and have wanted to do so for many years if only an effective financial arrangement could be found. They are aware of not being able to recruit a full social mix of pupils unless, as in the direct grant system, some support from public funds is made available to parents with low incomes and they would like to have this greater social mix, knowing it to be valuable both to the public schools themselves and to society. Although the girls' public schools can claim to recruit from a somewhat wider cross-section of children than some of the boys' public schools, the leading unendowed girls' public boarding schools, with their necessarily high fees and few available scholarships, are almost inevitably limited in their intake to pupils whose parents have relatively high incomes.

The public schools' desire to co-operate as far as is compatible with basic principles of independence, together with the strong political pressure from the present Labour Government to make some radical alterations of the *status quo*, is bound to force the issue—probably soon. We could arrive at the odd situation of the leading public schools being absorbed in some way into the state system, while the lesser independent schools flourish outside and meet a new set of needs based on criteria other than academic excellence.

There are two ways of looking at the future: what some of us think ought to happen and what seems likely to happen. The problems are of principle and of practice, the main practical problem being that of money. An extension of the direct grant system, with some extra help toward capital expenditure or capital borrowing would be the simplest method of linking the public with the maintained schools and at the same time giving the public schools the opportunity to develop so that the contribution they make can continue to be effective. The pooling idea, centrally controlled, could be combined with the direct grant principle to create some sound basis of financing and governing a scheme to pay for pupils sponsored by local authorities or by a central government department. There is no technical difficulty about this, only the seemingly overwhelming obstacle of lack of will of both central and local government, regardless of political party.

For myself, I take a wholly gloomy view of the prospects of this kind of development. I do not believe that any government in the foreseeable future could find sufficient support for setting aside a significant sum of public money to use in subsidizing the public schools in this way. At the same time I do not believe, passion, prejudice or cold reason notwithstanding, that any government could afford the cost of abolishing the public schools.

In 1965 the Department of Education and Science spent on the direct grant schools nearly £7 million in capitation and sixth-form grants and on remission of fees to parents. Local authorities spent £5 million on fees and grants. The figure arrived at earlier for taking up 25 per cent of secondary school places in recognized independent schools at local authority scales of payment for day school education was £9 million a year. This may seem a small amount out of a total education bill of some £1,700 million in the United Kingdom in 1965–66 but it is none the less a very large amount of money and few education or finance committees, whatever their party politics, would be likely to defend this.

The Public Schools Commission is asked to recommend ways in which the two systems could move nearer together.

Future of Girls' Public and Independent Schools

There will without doubt be local arrangements here and there where individual schools can work out schemes of collaboration for special purposes with neighbouring maintained schools, and there will, we may hope, be a widening of the concept of boarding 'need' which will bring more boys and girls from the maintained to the public boarding schools under arrangements similar to those that exist at present.

But if nothing much comes of all this, if the report of the Public Schools Commission finds its way, as many people already predict that it will, into the capacious maw of Departmental pigeon-holes-for-unimplementable-recommendations, what, *then*, is the future for the public schools?

We can take a passing glance at the trends in the United States. There, independent schools are more numerous in the older Eastern seaboard states than in the West, but even in California there is a large number of small, extremely expensive, wholly private academies. These schools usually take pupils of any ability, but they provide an intensely academic education and set out deliberately to fulfil parental ambitions to gain for their children places in the honours Ivy League universities, that is, the top ranking private prestige universities of Harvard, Yale, Princeton, Johns Hopkins and the rest. Failing this, these private schools or academies almost guarantee that they will place every pupil in some university or degree-awarding college. Classes in these schools are usually very small. In three schools of this kind which I visited in the United States in 1965 no teaching groups were larger than fifteen, and in the upper forms pupils had individual timetables and sometimes almost individual tuition. There is no shortage of teachers for these schools. Indeed one headmaster told me that he never advertises. Teachers with high qualifications write asking for posts—not because higher salaries are offered than can be earned in the public system, but because of the attractions of the small classes and the small school. Not all teachers like the very large schools that are the normal pattern in the USA. Pension schemes are interchangeable and, in any event, in the United States there is no common structure of teachers' salaries—each separate state (and even, within some states, each school district) sets its own scales for teachers' pay. The pupils themselves who have received this enormous privilege in teaching say that they feel at no social disadvantage when in due course they arrive at college. They soon get used to the huge numbers— the whole of American adult life is geared to large numbers anyway. No one asks or is the least bit interested in which school students have attended before coming to college; the only people who may know are former school colleagues and, if they are a sufficiently large group, they may perhaps form cliques. Their numbers are not, however, large enough for this to make any noticeable difference within the new college environment.

The indifference of American students once they are at college about where contemporaries have been to school is something that is also happening here. Young people after 18, whether at work or still in full-time education, are judged increasingly by what they are—what kind of a chap, what kind of a girl or more probably what kind of a bird. As secondary education recedes from its position of import- ance socially as the final stage of education, schools will become, from the point of view of the young people them- selves, of less *social* importance—just as now no one is the slightest bit interested socially whether someone they meet at university or at work attended as a child a private preparatory school or a maintained primary school.

In the United States some of the more famous women's university colleges find that they cannot recruit as many as half their intake of girls from the state schools. This is because academic achievement in the private schools in America is usually much higher than that of their state schools. The leading private girls' schools have standards comparable to those in an English grammar school, whereas academic work in American secondary high schools, at least until recently, has lagged some two years behind that of our grammar schools. The pattern is changing, especially since the panic which followed the successful launching by the Russians of the first Sputnik in 1957. Streaming on ability is being introduced into the American high schools for the first time: accelerated courses and advanced placement are becoming the new fashion. This may mean that the academic ascendance of the private schools will wane. On the other hand, new private academies are springing up everywhere throughout the South and in the big northern cities as the result of parents' reactions against the enforced desegregation of white and Negro children hitherto educated in separate schools.

American parents are now discovering that one or two years in the sixth forms of a British public boarding school for daughters who have had an 'accelerated education' in an American private academy can be a most successful venture; the sixth-form work here being of the standard of the average American women's liberal arts college. This is a new source of recruitment to British girls' public schools and enlivens the outlook of all the girls in a receiving school.

If in Britain the public schools are allowed to remain in existence but receive no financial help from public funds either for capital development or for sponsoring pupils, they will have to learn at least one important lesson from America. The schools will find themselves of necessity depending more even than now on appeals, and they will have to put aside all modesty, improve their public relations and go out begging in a businesslike and professional manner just as private schools and universities have to do in the United States. There they almost always employ experts to help them, or the principal himself becomes almost a professional appeals man. The British public schools will have to go not only to individual parents, and old boys' and old girls' associations, but to industry, commerce and professional bodies. This will strike horror in the hearts of the supporters of the girls' public schools, for experience has shown how difficult it is to raise money here for girls' schools or women's university colleges. The new women's college in Cambridge, New Hall, has had a tremendous struggle over a number of years to become well established: Churchill College for men, in new buildings near by, admittedly with an exceptional appeal, had several million pounds donated in a matter of months. The wealth of women's colleges in America can fill us with envy; but then women control more than half of all capital in America: in this country nothing like the same proportion.

AND NOW?

Meanwhile, what of the immediate future? The practical difficulties for parents in saving the money to send their children to the public schools, the high standards of design, accommodation and equipment in new maintained secondary schools and the financial problems of all the independent schools will cause the public schools to be under considerable pressures to come to any agreement that they can with the state system merely to survive. Schools with a strong denominational connection might be able to put increasingly high levies on church members and so carry on, subsidizing fees and meeting capital expenditure from central church funds as now. Some other schools might be able to band together into groups in order to reduce the costs of administration. Schools in the Allied Schools trust and in the Church Schools Association and the twenty-six direct grant schools of the Girls' Public Day School Trust are, for example, in a much stronger position to resist attrition than, in general, are those schools which stand alone.

Some public schools would be able to hold out come what may, putting up their fees year by year, becoming against their wishes more exclusive to the income groups from which they can draw their pupils, and increasing, through private appeals, the number of scholarships that they can offer. In this way they would gradually become the equivalent of the American academies described earlier. There is, however, a fundamental difference in this country. Firstly, the schools themselves do not want this. Secondly, the British public are probably more socialist-minded (across all political parties) than are the Americans. Our sense of what is fair precludes taking advantage of someone else because of having more money, whereas in America to be democratic is to be free to earn what one can and spend what one likes—and the more the better. Thirdly, we are very heavily taxed and we submit to being increasingly penalized as we move into higher income levels. Surtax and death duties have been and will continue to be the greatest enemies of the public schools, even if legacies could be freed of tax.

With education going on longer and a college or university education becoming more usual for those young people who have the ability and who do not have to rush into employment to keep families solvent, parents will be increasingly wary of committing themselves to high expenditure on their children's secondary education. When the secondary school was more often the terminal stage of education considerations were different. Better, now, some parents will think, to take what is free and save the money to help their children through subsidized higher education, particularly as many of them nowadays may want to have an extra year for a second degree, professional training, or other postgraduate research before taking up their first full-time paid posts.

A few public schools may be able to stand firm and know that they can weather any financial difficulties, taking as many sponsored pupils as they can persuade central government or local authorities to pay for, but going ahead in the certain knowledge that their prestige and renown is such that they can survive in any circumstances. Other schools may have to change radically. Their best chance is to concentrate on sixth-form work, to develop sixth-form houses or units or departments and to accept fee-paying 'students' for three-year, two-year or even one-year courses, even if this means taking in fewer pupils at the beginning of secondary education. This could change the whole pattern of a school, but it need not be catastrophic. There would be great attraction for some parents to send a girl away at 13 or 14 to a school that had at its summit a sixth-form unit which was tantamount to a college in itself. The schools may have to alter in balance of age groups, taking fewer at the younger ages to allow more provision for pupils from 16 to 18 even for non-academic courses.

Already some of the girls' schools are converting a boarding house or parts of their school buildings into separate units or 'student centres' for sixth-form girls. They feel that unless they do this they will not hold any girls into the second year of the sixth let alone a third year and therefore gradually these girls will lose in competition for university entrance with boys and girls from the leading maintained schools. As local authorities also begin to establish sixth-form colleges and to attach attractive sixth-form units to comprehensive schools, the idea is almost certain to become popular with the girls themselves, and, in the long run, what the pupils think is what counts most. However much those brought up in the tradition of the grammar schools may wish to resist this tendency to separate sixth forms from the full range of secondary education, they may find that the force of the new trend obliges them to give way. Specially designed sixth-form units within secondary schools will become accepted as normal and essential. Sixth-form colleges to which pupils come from other schools may also prove eventually to be an inescapable consequence of all-comprehensive systems if shortages of well-qualified specialist teaching staff grow. Those public schools which can find the money to develop the sixth-form unit idea quickly may more easily survive.

The girls' schools are now learning to accept that the girls in their care are, age for age, more grown up than they used to be. They are having to adjust rules and regulations so that the girls are treated more as adults. Many schools are discarding school uniform at least for the older girls and out of school, and they are all increasing the privileges afforded to sixth formers. Some schools are abandoning prefect systems and giving girls considerable say in managing school affairs. There has to be some restriction on freedom outside school, more perhaps nowadays in the motor-car age than in years gone by—the schools are, after all, *in loco parentis*; truancy too, now frequent in some of the maintained day schools, could lead to serious trouble if it occurred from a girls' boarding school. The schools are having to give further thought to weekly boarding, and to allowing full boarders greater freedom to go home during term time, even though this may lessen the strength of the school's corporate life and the use that the boarding schools have traditionally made of Sundays in general cultural development as well as religious observance. They are having to recognize that girls are far more adult in their relationship with boys than they were allowed or expected to be, or even thought of being, a short generation ago. Girls at boarding schools are being allowed to go to shops (usually during specified hours only) and to meet friends outside schools. Wherever possible and suitable, girls are nowadays allowed to visit the cinema, the theatre, and attend public concerts. An imaginative use of television for both education and entertainment is essential nowadays in any school. The difficulties of making all these freedoms possible are great. How to fit everything in when timetables are sometimes already too full and competition for university places makes concentration on study necessary is certainly a problem, but solutions have to be found—through flexibility, good management and a ruthless pruning of inessential routines. All this requires great imagination on the part of every member of a boarding school's staff.

Wherever a school is in the vicinity of a university or other college, as great co-operation as possible needs to be and usually nowadays is fostered in literary, music, art, scientific societies and other activities; girls in public boarding schools as well as in day schools are being given time and encouragement to join in games and other outdoor and leisure pursuits with pupils in neighbouring maintained schools, in shared projects involving social work in youth clubs and the like. Most of the girls' public schools take part in these activities, but some could perhaps do more. Public schools as a whole cannot survive any longer in total exclusiveness and isolation.

A few could do so, if permitted, by becoming increasingly expensive and socially selective, but they must all, as so many of them already do, learn from the new ideas which are proving successful, particularly with the less able girls, in the maintained schools. The girls' public schools are already accepting today's greater social equalities; they are already modifying their sometimes too treasured exclusiveness and giving, in every way that they can invent, to the community outside the school walls, even at the expense of some loss of time for study and for school and house activities. They combine in educational experiments such as closed circuit television teaching, they share science teachers and laboratories, explore common new syllabuses, projects, new examinations and the rest. Some are better placed than others to be able to contribute—the more they are able to do the more they add to their own stature, attractiveness and strength as well as giving from their own wealth of experience to the wider world of the maintained schools.

The public schools have not pioneered secondary education over the centuries and particularly over the past hundred years only to be snuffed out now. This is a great moment of truth and of decision for them. Either they will be forced by financial circumstances into becoming more exclusive which they do not want to happen, or, while holding firmly to independence where they think fit, they must join generously in the main stream of education in this country as, indeed, they desire to do and many are doing. If they can overcome their financial difficulties in the course of this collaboration, they will assuredly move into a new era of their history. The dice need not always then be loaded against them. It is not beyond the wit of an educated community, recognizing before it is too late the value of an enterprising and vigorous independent or near-independent system of education running parallel with the state system, to devise some financial scheme whereby the independent schools are not irrevocably priced out of existence. Have we not a new binary system of higher education invented astonishingly by a Labour Secretary of State? If this is possible, anything is possible.

There is no necessity to give way about independence. The retention of an independent governing body was the first of the six principles formulated by representatives of the girls' public schools. An alert governing body with an effective and knowledgeable chairman can be a great source of strength to a school—indeed, the future of each individual independent or public school depends on both heads and members of governing bodies. Men and women who are prepared to identify themselves with the schools, who understand the problems and, voluntarily, give time and thought to resolving them, are the schools' principal ambassadors. There was a time when their duties may have seemed light—a governors' meeting now and again, perhaps a finance or house committee, a speech day and an annual report. But now the schools are being closely examined by a major government commission—if this time of trial does nothing else it will help us to see ourselves as others see us and to reassess our role in the national system of education and to make changes where desirable of our own volition.

Parental choice is without doubt being steadily narrowed. Those of us who believe in freedom and who are prepared to pay a high price to increase choice as a matter of principle where the upbringing of our children is concerned need to be awake to the dangers. We can too easily become brainwashed into supposing that anything which would further our own ideas of freedom of choice would necessarily be detrimental to the majority who do not have the same burning desire to preserve independence wherever possible. Most of us have caught the habit of accepting that every increase in taxation to meet rising costs and standards of public welfare services is necessarily inevitable. An increasingly powerful welfare state can bring its own forms of mesmerism almost without our being aware of this. The needs of the majority must come first, but these are not necessarily incompatible with the co-existence of minority freedoms; if we are to preserve these at all, some new approach may be essential—soon. The independent schools are unlikely to be able to help the lower income families as much as the better off, but they do give parents the freedom to decide how to spend on their children's education what is left of their own money after all taxes are paid.

The schools have to demonstrate to a wider public that they are in touch with modern trends. Governors must wake up to the dangers that threaten and realize that this is now a moment to do or die and that time is no longer on the side of their schools. Headmasters and headmistresses will have to make great efforts and exercise considerable powers of imagination to see how best they can mould valuable traditions to meet new situations, and then publicize—even advertise—the changes that have been made. The girls' public schools have a history of achievement on which a new future of unassailable worth can be built. With their independence, high academic standards and special understanding of the needs of girls they are uniquely well placed to provide the education which many parents seek for their daughters.

Basic to all the foregoing discussion is the belief in the fundamental right of parents to be able, as far as is reasonable, to choose the kind of education which they want for their children—provided that in doing so they do not deprive others. No one has yet put forward any evidence that if there were no girls' public and other independent schools then state education would thereby be better. If teaching staffs were disbanded, many women would give up teaching and there would be little compensating gain in graduate women teachers in the state system. There is little if any evidence of social divisiveness caused by the girls' public schools. They offer an education deliberately orientated toward service to the community—other schools do so too, but the public schools should not be castigated for their traditional success in this.

Parents must show faith in the schools and not be too intimidated by political pressures. We do not have to bow without protest to dictatorships even when these are disguised as democracy. If we want a free society enough, if we care enough for the possibility of still having independent schools, we can have them.

There are avenues for action by everyone. My own active interest in education was first aroused by being elected some sixteen years ago a governor of my public school and later by becoming a co-opted member of my local education committee. Not everyone can give the time that this kind of involvement tends eventually to take up, but by forming parents' associations or societies of 'friends of the schools', all who have an interest can play a part. Parent-teacher associations which are welcomed by some heads of maintained schools are probably not appropriate for public schools, but parents' associations are different and parents of some leading girls' public schools have already banded themselves together to form strong and effective associations. Most of the girls' public schools have old girls' associations which can be a powerful influence: some might usefully extend their organizations to include past and present parents whether old girls or not; the help that could be given by fathers would bring a new source of strength. Affiliation to some new national association of friends of the girls' public schools might also be effective in protecting the fundamental right of parents to be able to choose as far as possible the education that they wish for their children.

But if we are content to join the ranks of the don't knows, to go along with what is handed out to us (albeit paid for in taxes by us), to submit to the notion that other people know more about what is best for our children than we do ourselves—in short, if, by default, we allow freedom to choose the education that we wish for our children to be whittled away, then we shall have to accept what the politicians and the experts decree. We must not then be surprised if we wake up one day to find that, along with some other excellences of the past, the public schools have disappeared.

APPENDIX

Public Schools Commission—Terms of Reference

The main function of the Commission will be to advise on the best way of integrating the public schools with the state system of education. For the immediate purpose of the Commission public schools are defined as those independent schools now in membership of the Headmasters' Conference, Governing Bodies' Association or Governing Bodies of Girls' Schools Association.

The Commission will be expected to carry out the following tasks:

(a) To collect and assess information about the public schools and about the need and existing provision for boarding education; forms of collaboration between the schools (in the first instance the boarding schools) and the maintained system.

(b) To work out the role which individual schools might play in national and local schemes of integration.

(c) If it so wishes, and subject to the approval of the Secretary of State, to initiate experimental schemes matching existing provision with different types of need.

(*d*) To recommend a national plan for integrating the schools with the maintained sector of education.

(*e*) To recommend whether any action is needed in respect of other independent schools, whether secondary or primary.

In carrying out its tasks the Commission will be expected (while respecting the denominational character of the schools), to pay special attention to the following objectives:

(*a*) To ensure that the public schools should make their maximum contribution to meeting national educational needs, and in the first instance any unsatisfied need for boarding education in the light of the Martin* and Newsom† Reports.

(*b*) To create a socially mixed entry into the schools in order both to achieve (*a*) above and to reduce the divisive influence which they now exert.

(*c*) To move towards a progressively wider range of academic attainment amongst public school pupils, so that the public school sector may increasingly conform with the national policy for the maintained sector.

(*d*) To co-operate closely with local education authorities in seeking to match provision with need for boarding education.

(*e*) To ensure the progressive application of the principle that the public schools, like other parts of the educational system, should be open to boys and girls irrespective of the income of their parents.

* Report of the Working Party on Assistance with the Cost of Boarding Education, published 1960.

† *Half Our Future*—A report of the Central Advisory Council for Education (England), published 1963.

GLOSSARY

Aided Schools: A voluntary school whose managers are responsible for repairs to the exterior of the building, and for capital expenditure for alterations required by the local education authority to bring the premises up to the standards of the Building Regulations. All running costs are met by the authority; capital costs of improvement and repair to external fabric are eligible for 80 per cent Exchequer grant. The managers have substantial rights in the appointment and dismissal of teachers and in giving denominational religious education. One-third of the managers are appointed by the local education authority.

All-age School: A school containing pupils for the full range of primary education and for part or all of compulsory secondary education.

B.Ed.: Degree of Bachelor of Education. A degree in education proposed by the Committee on Higher Education to be awarded after a four-year course.

Building Programme: A list of projects on which the Department will allow building to start in a particular financial year. The total value of the programme is determined in advance according to the predicted educational demands and the capital investment available, and allocations are made to local education authorities as far in advance as possible, to enable them to begin planning.

Burnham Committee (properly the Burnham Primary and Secondary Committee): A committee consisting of representatives of teachers, local education authorities and the Secretary of State for Education and Science, which negotiates teachers' salaries.

Glossary

Capitation Allowance: Annual allowance allocated by local education authorities in respect of each pupil for expenditure by schools on consumable materials, equipment, books and the like.

CLASP: A consortium of local education authorities co-operating in the design and building of schools and in the design and marketing of school furniture and equipment.

Comprehensive School: A secondary school intended to cater for the secondary education of all the pupils in an area, organized as a whole and not in clearly defined grammar, modern and technical sides. In Circular 10/65, The Secretary of State requested local education authorities to submit plans for reorganizing secondary education on comprehensive lines.

Controlled School: A voluntary school for which the local education authority is financially responsible. The authority appoints two-thirds of the managers as compared with one-third in aided schools. Although controlled schools follow an 'Agreed Syllabus' parents may opt for not more than two periods a week of denominational instruction. Teachers necessary to give this denominational instruction—'reserved teachers'—may be appointed for the purpose.

County School: A school which is built, maintained and staffed by the local education authority. Its full cost falls on public funds.

CSE: Certificate of Secondary Education. A subject examination taken at the end of a five-year course of secondary education.

Direct Grant School: A school receiving maintenance grants directly from the Exchequer in return for which 25 per cent of its places are offered free mainly through local education authorities to pupils who have attended a maintained school for not less than two years. The remainder of the places may be available for fee payers, except that a further 25 per cent must be made available to the authority if they wish to take them up. For full description see Chapter IV.

Eleven-plus (*11* +) : The conventional term used to cover the techniques (e.g. attainment or intelligence tests) which a local education authority may use to allocate pupils leaving primary schools at or about the age of 11 to different types of secondary education.

First School: Term to be used for a school for the 5 to 8 year age group (or 5 to 9).

Form Entry: The number of classes or 'forms' admitted in a year.

GCE: General Certificate of Education. A subject examination normally taken at the end of a five-year course of secondary education ('Ordinary level') and at the end of a seven-year course ('Advanced level').

Governors: Members of a governing body of a secondary school or college.

Graded Post: A post of responsibility which carries an allowance additional to the basic salary scale.

Hadow Reports: Reports of the Consultative Committee under the Chairmanship of Sir Henry Hadow. They were: *The Education of the Adolescent* (1926), *The Primary School* (1931) and *Infant and Nursery Schools* (1933).

Independent School: A school which is not supported out of public funds, providing primary or secondary education or both. (See also *Recognized*.)

Glossary

Maintained School: A county or voluntary school maintained by a local education authority.

Middle School: A school for children aged 8 to 12 (or 9 to 13).

Nuffield Foundation: An independent trust which has sponsored research and development in various fields. Currently sponsoring projects in French, mathematics and science in primary schools in collaboration with the Schools Council.

Oversized Classes: Classes containing more pupils than laid down in the Department's Regulations, that is 30 for nursery classes in primary schools or for senior pupils in all-age schools, 40 in other primary schools and 30 in secondary schools.

Primary School: School at present catering for children under 12.

Quota: A system designed to alleviate maldistribution of teachers. Local education authorities are assigned by the Department of Education and Science a total number of full-time teachers for staffing their schools which they are not expected to exceed.

Recognized as Efficient: All independent schools must be registered by the Department of Education and Science which lays down certain minimum standards. Schools can apply to be 'recognized as efficient' under the Department's Rule 16. Recognition is only granted to schools achieving much more stringent standards.

Registered: See *Recognized as Efficient.*

Schools Council for the Curriculum and Examinations: A body set up in 1964 jointly by local authority and teacher associations and the Department of Education and Science.

Glossary

School-leaving Age: Date at which compulsory education ends, at present the Easter or Summer after a pupil's fifteenth birthday. The leaving age is to be raised to 16 in 1970–71.

Secondary School: School at present catering for children over 11.

Selective School: School for which pupils can be selected, usually at 11 plus, on the grounds that they would benefit from a more academic education than is provided in non-selective schools.

Setting: Division of an age group into different groups or sets for some subjects according to ability in those subjects.

Voluntary School: A school which can be built by a voluntary body, for example, a denomination, but which is maintained by a local education authority. (See *Aided* and *Controlled Schools.*)

Index

Index

Index

Index

Index